Paradise ON ICE

50 FABULOUS TROPICAL COCKTAILS
BY MITTIE HELLMICH

CHRONICLE BOOKS
SAN FRANCISCO

DEDICATION:

In memory of my mother, Susan Hellmich Pierce, whose boundless generosity always brought a warmth and elegance, creative flair, and *joie de vivre* to any gathering, she remains my constant inspiration.

ACKNOWLEDGMENTS

No woman is an island. I had the good fortune to be surrounded by a sea of generously creative family and friends, and to have the best editorial experts and savvy design team in the business. I am indebted to the following people for their part in producing this slice of paradise: Bill LeBlond, editor extraordinaire and tropical visionary, for his wisdom, guidance, and patience; his sharp assistant, Amy Treadwell; and meticulously fabulous copy editor Sharon Silva. Vivien Sung and her design team, for assembling the archipelago of photographic imagery with a finely tuned eye, bringing a visual elegance to the subject matter. Karen Brooks, for her infinite wisdom, editorial input, moral support, and brilliant advice in many realms and, most importantly, her sophisticatedly savage wit that humored me through many a daunting moment. Gideon Bosker, whose savvy cultural insights and creative energy are a constant source of inspiration, for his expert advice and boundless encouragement, guidance, and support, and for graciously lending his lush locales and impeccable taste for photographic purposes. Nicole Hudson Pierce Rhoads, for her exquisite photo-styling finesse and photo-assistant skills delivered with a saint-like patience, and for her priceless witticisms and moral support. Nick Pierce and Donna Peterson, for being the gracious hosts of a perfectly balmy photographic location, as well as for their adept styling panache, photographic assistance, and fine weather acumen. Catherine Glass, for her superfine editing skills that put a polish on the ice in paradise. Amanda Wurzbach, for her in-depth research assistance and Martha touches. Geoff Rhoads, Taylor James Pierce, Masha Turchinsky, Edwardo Gustamante, Bryan Rhoads, Janet Keating, and Mark Miller for their editorial input, sipping insights, brainstorming and proofreading skills, moral support, and advice. Trevor, Amanda, and Hugo Rhoads—the best non-alcoholic tasting experts that an aunt could ever hope for. Dirk and Lisa Pierce, for sharing their perfected tropical taste-testing experiences. Tim Evans and Michele Nimon, those creative cocktail alchemists who fearlessly sipped for the cause. Lara Turchinsky, for sharing her cocktail secrets. Nita and Theo Pozzy, for hosting tropical cocktail testing soires with style, along with Ladd and Lynne McKittrick, for bringing their discerning palates. The guys at Uptown Liquor store—my spirit gurus.

Text and photographs copyright © 2002 by Mittie Hellmich. All rights reserved. No part of this book may be reproduced in any form without written permission from the publisher.

Printed in Singapore

Library of Congress
Cataloging-in-Publication Data:
Hellmich, Mittie, 1960–
Paradise on ice : 50 fabulous tropical cocktails / by Mittie Hellmich.
  p. cm.
Includes index.
ISBN 0-8118-3302-X
Cocktails. I. Title.
TX951.H45 2002
641.8'74—dc21
    2001037238

Designed by **tom & john**: A DESIGN COLLABORATIVE, SF

Flowers and other accessories in the drink photos are for decoration only and are not edible.

Distributed in Canada by Raincoast Books
9050 Shaughnessy Street
Vancouver, BC V6P 6E5

10 9 8 7 6 5 4 3 2 1

Chronicle Books LLC
85 Second Street
San Francisco, California 94105

www.chroniclebooks.com

Contents

INTRODUCTION

Whatever modern-life obsession you've chosen to pour yourself into, admit it, you're secretly yearning for an easy, breezy segue—an escape hatch from your kinetic, mind-reeling urban existence. What you wouldn't give for a taste of life in the languid lane, for the feel of fine sand beneath your feet, for a day of sun-drenched meditation on whether to crack open a coconut or gather seashells—all chased with a liquid ambrosia so rich it registers way off the Richter scale of decadence.

Paradise on Ice can't buy you an airline ticket to the Bahamas. But these tropical tonics can transport you straight to that hammock of the mind: a palm-festooned island of white-hot beaches where an unexpected romantic rendezvous unfolds under a night sky so packed with stars that you're looking for the dance floor. In other words, whatever your fantasy, this slim volume has it covered.

Enter drinks from the paradise zone. Here you'll find such sublime classics as the refreshing mojito, with its vivacious Cuban crush of fresh mint, lime, and rum; and the sultry Dark and Stormy, a Bermuda specialty of molasses-rich island rum and bubbly ginger brew; plus a slew of fruity-licious elixirs made with every tropical juice known to Tarzan and Jane. And that doesn't even begin to address the world of frosty daiquiris, zesty margaritas, and creamy piña coladas. What you have here, in a coco-nutshell, is a repertoire of libations to lounge by.

The most intriguing tropical drinks are inspired by the innovations in today's savvy mixology scene. As local supermarkets have gone global, the variety of exotic traveling fruits and juices has opened up the exploration of a whole new palate of flavors, from the strawberry-honey–like guava to the

4

densely sweet mango to the delicately fragrant lychee. When combined with traditional tropical spirits and liqueurs, the result is a rethinking of the classics and a whole new wave of fun recipes. A gin martini with a whisper of passion fruit, for example, will be the buzz of your next summer party. Or, consider giving your friends a taste of island euphoria by mixing up a frosty pitcher of papaya margaritas infused with the heavenly scent of Damiana liqueur.

When you're in the mood to play the adventurous alchemist, try whipping up some sumptuous homemade infusions for adding depth and complexity to your drinks. Steeping aromatic ingredients like pineapple or ginger in rum, tequila, or vodka creates a whole new level of delicious flavors. These infused liquors add a lush dimension to such contemporary creations as the Madagascar Mood Shifter, a West Indies spin on the margarita using tangerine juice and vanilla-infused tequila, or use them as a springboard for your own creations. Don't worry if your high-school chemistry course ended in a literal blast. The infusions are simple to make and well worth the effort.

Naturally, this collection pays homage to those legendary figures whose personal quest for the perfect thirst quencher effectively catapulted the magic of the tropics onto the cultural landscape. *Paradise on Ice* offers tongue-tingling re-creations of the sassy Brazilian caipirinha; the Hemingway daiquiri, created at El Floridita, the writer's favorite Havana watering hole; and the Ramos brothers' Gin Fizz, a frothy Gulf Coast drink

tinged with orange water. You'll discover the madness behind the methods in the tiki zone, where Don the Beachcomber sprung the notoriously potent Zombie and Trader Vic Bergeron unleashed the equally powerful mai tai on an unsuspecting world.

Such signature drinks return us to the spirit of the fantasy-driven Polynesian pleasure domes of the West Coast in the late 1940s and early 1950s. Among them was the first Trader Vic's, where the upscale clientele sucked on Samoan Fog Cutters while contentedly cocooned in a décor blueprinted from the South Seas. The elaborate libations had a reputation for holding enough spirits to light a tiki torch and enough plastic flora and fauna to give birth to the whole notion of kitsch. At the ultra-glam Cocoanut Grove, another hot spot, the famous and infamous alike created fodder for gossip columnists as they moved to the rumba beat of the Xavier Cugat Orchestra, all the while keeping cool with a barful of exotic cocktails.

Ultimately, this collection of sun-kissed elixirs captures the spirit of the tropics without you ever having to leave your backyard. From papaya margaritas to mandarin daiquiris to spirit-free fruit smoothies, these inspired concoctions are guaranteed to make your summer dance party, beach blanket bash, suave soirée, or moonlight encounter the next best thing to a breezy island existence.

In *Paradise on Ice*, the modern tropical cocktail has arrived. Let the fun—and the limbo—begin.

Tools of the Tropics

To structure a glass of perfected equatorial bliss takes only a few basic bar skills: how to shake a cocktail, frost a glass, sculpt an enviable garnish, and recognize the distinguishing characteristics of various rums and tequilas. Equipment is minimal. Only a small battery of bar accessories is needed to produce your island concoction. This section has all the necessary tips and tools, from a complete guide to exotic fruits to the secrets of preparing a lime-zest rim. Follow the helpful instructions and you will be on the inside track to becoming an accomplished tropical drinkologist in the paradise lounge.

Island Accessories

When one conjures up a picture of tropical living, an element of unwavering simplicity is inevitably part of its charm. In other words, as seductive as that flashy, high-tech bar equipment may be, in my experience the only tools you really need are a paring knife, a jigger, a cocktail shaker or blender, and two glasses in which to pour your fabulous fizz. The following list has all the essentials you will need to shake it up, island style.

BAR SPOON

For stirring tall, noncarbonated drinks, muddling ingredients, and measuring spoonfuls of sugar. Look for a skinny, long-handled spoon with a small bowl.

BLENDER

A must-have item for fruity frappés and daiquiris. The ideal cocktail blender has a powerful motor, is able to crush ice and to puree fruit, and has a stainless-steel container for a quick chill.

CITRUS JUICER

This simple but effective gadget will save you from tiresome hand-squeezing, a boon when you are entertaining. Depending on your budget, you can go for a simple reamer in plastic or glass or an electric model for high-volume juicing.

COCKTAIL SHAKER

The beauty of this hip, elegant, and essential bar tool is in the simplicity of its make, shake, and strain quickness. There are quite a few style options from which to choose, but the best shaker for mixing and chilling a drink is the classic stainless-steel canister with a built-in strainer and a tightly fitted top.

FINE-MESH METAL STRAINER

This tool, also known as a sieve, comes in handy for straining out unwanted fruit pulp, seeds, or peel when preparing infusions and syrups.

JIGGER/PONY AND SHOT GLASS

For the gizmo inclined, there is the classic double-ended measure of the jigger/pony. This small hourglass-shaped tool will typically have a 1 1/2-ounce measure (1 jigger; standard cocktail amount) on one end and a 1-ounce measure (the pony) on the other. An equally handy alternative is the shot glass, with the best ones having gradations indicating 1/2 ounce to 1 1/2 or 2 ounces—priceless when perfecting a drink.

ICE BUCKET

Another completely functional—and fabulous-looking—accessory to add to your bar service. A range of styles are available, from retro chrome to elegant glass to practical and thermal, with a lid to keep the ice from melting too quickly and a pair of metal or plastic tongs to wrangle your cubes.

MIXING PITCHER OR GLASS

A tall 16-ounce glass pitcher is great for stirring crystal-clear martinis or Manhattans and for mixing more than two drinks at a time. The ideal pitcher has a pinched, molded lip that holds back the ice when you pour. If you prefer to use a pint-sized mixing glass, be sure to have a circular wire metal bar strainer to fit over the top for pouring.

MUDDLER

A wooden stick with a broad, rounded base used to muddle, that is, crush, limes and sugar and dozens of other ingredients in a glass, to release their essence.

PARING KNIFE

A tool used for most of the detail cutting, from garnish preparation to slicing ingredients like ginger and small fruits.

STIRRING ROD

Made of glass or plastic, and typically found as one-half of a glass mixing-pitcher set, it is used to stir classic martinis and carbonated liquids.

SWIZZLE STICK

Great for fishing out garnishes and for stirring things up, this indispensable item comes in an assortment of materials and styles, from kitschy plastic wands that recall Trader Vic's Polynesian scene to classy slender silver models.

VEGETABLE PEELER AND ZESTER/STRIPPER

The peeler is a handy tool for removing large strips of citrus peel, while the zester/stripper (a sharp metal tool with a row of tiny holes at one end) is essential for producing fine threads of zest.

Techniques from the Tiki Bar

ARTFUL DRINKOLOGY
From the spirits all the way down to the juice, a drink is only as good as its ingredients. In other words, use the best that is available and that your pocketbook will allow. For example, a daiquiri made with first-rate rum deserves fresh lime juice and fresh fruit to keep the quality level high. This is true of all drinks, but you can be selective. A medium-priced tequila will hold up in a mixed drink with a festival of flavors. Save that expensive añejo tequila for a martini, a highball, or for sipping.

MEASURING UP
Leave the eyeballing to the professionals. (I have a sneaking suspicion their drinks taste different every time anyway.) The best way to arrive at the intended result of the perfected recipe is to use a jigger in a precise manner—this is like chemistry, after all. Only then will you be spared the cocktail that doesn't quite hit the right note.

SUAVE SHAKING
The quickest way to look like a master mixologist is to shake those cocktails in a shimmering blur of chrome. As a rule, drinks using cloudier ingredients such as sugar, cream, fruit juices, and liqueurs are best shaken, since they need vigorous movement to blend well. To shake a drink in the standard shaker, put a glassful of cracked ice in the base,

add the ingredients, put the cap in place, and then top with the lid. Grasp with both hands, one holding the lid on, and shake to blend and chill the ingredients. Don't be shy. Shake like the percussionist in a world-class salsa band. Take the lid off and strain the drink through the built-in strainer in the cap into the appropriate glass.

SULTRY STIRRING
There is something undeniably romantic about that tinkling sound produced when a drink is stirred with ice. Simultaneously, the crystal clear liquid is chilled and the glass pitcher is lost in frost. Drinks made of clear ingredients, like the gin martini, Champagne cocktail, and juleps, are meant for stirring. Also, shaking anything with bubbles will flatten the effervescence and cloud the clear, pure liquors. Put a handful of ice cubes in the pitcher (warning, the pinched lip won't hold back cracked ice), pour the liquor over the ice, and stir firmly to chill. Pour into a chilled glass.

TO CHILL A GLASS
Prechilled glasses from the freezer are the best way to keep your drinks cold. Rinsing a glass in cold water and then chilling it in the freezer for an hour or so will give it the proper frosty patina. If you need a chilled glass pronto, fill the glass with cracked ice and cold water and chill it while you're mixing the drinks. Toss out the ice, wipe out any excess water, and pour in the drink. If you have fine crystal, chill it in the refrigerator or by the ice-cube chilling method to avoid cracking the glass.

Glassware

Glasses come in countless designs, styles, and colors, but unless you are a glass-collecting fanatic, your repertoire doesn't have to be extensive, only functional. Serving the right cocktail in the right glass is part of the ritual, but a few basic styles will see you through many types of drinks: a 4- to 6-ounce cocktail glass, a 12- to 14-ounce Collins glass, and an 8- to 10-ounce Old-Fashioned glass.

CHAMPAGNE FLUTE
Tall, thin stemmed, and elegant, this 6- to 8-ounce glass has a narrow bowl opening specifically for preserving the effervescence in Champagne.

COCKTAIL GLASS
The 4- to 6-ounce cocktail glass is similar to the martini glass, but it has a slightly more rounded bowl. Meant for cocktails served "up," or without ice, it is used interchangeably with the martini glass.

HIGHBALL OR COLLINS GLASS
Highball glasses come in a range of sizes, anywhere from 8 to 10 ounces to a taller 10- to 14-ounce glass also known as a chimney. Frequently interchangeable with the highball is the 10- to 14-ounce Collins glass. This tall tumbler is usually filled with ice and a frosty, fizzy cooler. The classic Zombie cocktail is served in a larger 16-ounce version.

HURRICANE GLASS
Short stemmed and with a slight curve in the body fashioned after the shape of a hurricane lamp, this glass will hold 16 to 20 ounces of your favorite rum punch.

IRISH COFFEE GLASS

This heatproof, 8- to 10-ounce glass, for serving a hot toddy or buttered rum, is usually made of clear, tempered glass and is outfitted with a handle or with a base and handle of stainless steel.

MARGARITA GLASS

Besides the margarita, this 6- to 8-ounce festive dessert bowl on a stem is great for any frozen, blended concoction. You can use a large wine goblet in its place.

MARTINI GLASS

This is a 4- to 6-ounce glass with an iconic shape: a flared, open top and a thin, elegant stem. It's perfect for those clear, jewel-colored elixirs served "up."

OLD-FASHIONED GLASS

The 8- to 10-ounce straight-edged, short, stocky tumbler, also known as a rocks glass, should have a heavy bottom that will stand up to muddling your mint or lime. This sturdy glass is ideally suited for drinks served over ice.

SHOT GLASS

This sturdy 1 1/2- to 2-ounce glass is meant for tossing back an ounce of straight spirits or for layered shooters. It is available in an endless variety of fun styles.

Liquid Measurements

Bar spoon = $1/2$ oz

1 teaspoon = $1/6$ oz

1 tablespoon = $1/2$ oz

2 tablespoons (pony) = 1 oz

3 tablespoons (jigger) = 1 $1/2$ oz

$1/4$ cup = 2 oz

$1/3$ cup = 3 oz

$1/2$ cup = 4 oz

$2/3$ cup = 5 oz

$3/4$ cup = 6 oz

1 cup = 8 oz

1 pint = 16 oz

1 quart = 32 oz

750 ml bottle = 25.4 oz

1 liter bottle = 33.8 oz

1 medium lemon = 3 tablespoons juice

1 medium lime = 2 tablespoons juice

1 medium orange = $1/3$ cup juice

Fruitropia and Other Lush Bounty from the Islands

When it comes to defining the tropical drink, fruit juices and fresh fruits are essential in pursuit of that sunshine-in-a-glass experience. From coconuts and papayas to mangoes and kumquats, this *fruits du soleil* glossary will prepare the tropical-drink connoisseur for squeezing, mixing, and carving the fruits used to create a paradise on ice. A few other ingredients indispensable to the tropical bar are tucked in among the fruits.

Ripe fresh fruit or freshly squeezed juice will always give you the best flavor, of course. But when a fruit is out of season, frozen whole and cut fruits and purees are readily available in most supermarkets. For party preparation, or just for convenience, you can cut up or puree large amounts of ripe fruit and freeze them for later use. Extracting the usable flesh of some fruits, like the seed-filled guava, can present a challenge. In these cases, juice or frozen pulp is a practical alternative. Fortunately, supermarkets and specialty grocers are steadily improving at stocking a wide variety of exotic fruits.

The recipes in this book call for fruits that are easily accessible in one form or another, whether juice or nectar, fresh, frozen, or pureed.

Rules of thumb:

- *Look for unblemished fruit that is close to ripe or is ripe.*

- *Never refrigerate unripe fruit.*

- *Wash fruit prior to using, but never before that.*

BANANA

The potassium-rich yellow banana is the fruit of a tropical plant that grows most commonly in warm, humid climes. Unlike most fruits, bananas develop a better flavor when they are ripened off the bush, so they are harvested when they are bright green. A banana ripe and ready to use will be fragrant and flecked with tiny brown specks. Although many exotic varieties exist, the Cavendish is the most common and is readily available year-round.

To prepare: Peel the skin back, exposing the creamy, edible flesh. To use in blended drinks, slice the banana crosswise, or put the whole, peeled banana in a plastic bag in the freezer to slice up later.

CANTALOUPE

Americans call the muskmelon a cantaloupe, although there is another Italian melon that is botanically known as the cantaloupe. In season during the summer months, cantaloupes are heavy for their size, comparable to that of a small bowling ball. A ripe cantaloupe is one that smells sweet; is peach colored under the textured, grayish beige netting of its rind; and is soft at both ends when pressed.

To prepare: Slice the melon in half and remove the cluster of tiny white seeds at the center. Scoop or slice the vibrant orange flesh from the rind. Cut into cubes and enjoy in your favorite blended daiquiri or margarita.

COCONUT

The star of so many deserted-island scenarios, the shaggy brown coconut, with its interior of pure white meat, is actually the core of the mature nut. In its whole form, the brown, furry sphere is surrounded by a large, green football of fibrous husk. In some Latin markets, vendors will lop the tops off these enormous fruits with a machete, accessing the sweet coconut water and white, custardlike inside for an instant treat. With further aging, the white flesh becomes the crisp white meat of the coconut interior. When you shake a coconut, you should hear liquid sloshing inside, and the "eyes" (the three small, round dark spots at one end of the nut) should be dry. Look for these tropical icons year-round at the market, with the peak season in early fall through December.

The ritual of opening a coconut is labor intensive. Using the fresh coconut meat is unnecessary, since shredded dried coconut, coconut cream, coconut milk, and coconut water are widely available. Coconut cream, sometimes labeled "cream of coconut," is a canned, sweetened product used primarily for desserts and tropical drinks. Coconut milk (not to be confused with coconut cream, nor with the water from the coconut) is made from the pureed coconut meat and is not particularly sweet. It is sold in cans, and imports from Thailand, such as Thai Kitchen brand, are best. For a lighter alternative, Goya has a great coconut-water beverage. You can find these ingredients either in the ethnic-foods section of the supermarket, or in Latin or Asian markets.

To prepare: If you are serving your drink in a hollowed-out coconut half or otherwise garnishing your creation, look for "easy crack" coconuts, that is, coconuts that have been scored around the center. With a pointed, sharp instrument—an ice pick works well—and a hammer, pierce the eyes and drain the coconut water into a glass. Crack open the shell by tapping it with a hammer at the scored line, or if you have a nonscored coconut, wrap it in a towel and whack it a few times to break it open. Cut out the white flesh with a knife, then cut any leathery brown skin off the pieces. Shave off paper-thin slices or grate with a handheld grater for garnishes.

GINGER

Ginger is technically the rhizome of a tropical plant, a versatile root that is used fresh, dried, powdered, or pickled in a multitude of ways. It is an especially popular addition to drinks in Jamaica, where it's used to make ginger beer and ginger tea. Ginger can be found fresh in most produce sections. Sliced or grated, it infuses a cocktail with a sweet, spicy flavor.

To prepare: Peel away the thin brown skin, then slice with a sharp knife or grate on the fine rasps of a handheld grater.

GRAPEFRUIT

The color of the grapefruit's flesh varies depending on the variety and where it was grown. Some grapefruits have a whitish or pale yellow flesh, while others range from pink to a deep red. All varieties have a primarily yellow rind, although some rinds exhibit a pinkish blush. Fresh grapefruit is available year-round. Fresh grapefruit juice is always preferable in drink recipes, mainly because grapefruit juice concentrates, liquid or frozen, tend to be more bitter than fresh grapefruit juice.

To prepare: Cut the grapefruit in half and juice it in an electric juicer or by hand. Most grapefruits have a handful of large seeds that will come out during juicing. They should be discarded.

GUANABANA

Also known as soursop in the Caribbean, this fruit native to South America has smooth, greenish brown skin (some may have a slight texture), creamy white flesh, and an interesting flavor mix of sweet and sour. Rarely found in North American markets in their fresh state, guanabanas are available in Latin markets either in frozen pulp form or as a juice. Goya puts out a fine guanabana nectar.

To prepare: With a sharp paring knife, peel the skin off, cut in half to remove the black seeds, and cut the flesh into cubes to use in batido *smoothies, or freeze for future use.*

GUAVA

The guava is a favorite in the tropical-fruit cornucopia. This egg-shaped fruit, fragrant and sweet with flavors that recall honey, strawberry, and melon, is available from October through March. Many varieties exist, ranging in skin color from dark green to red, yellow, and even shades of purple and black. To be eaten raw, guavas should be very ripe. Choose one that feels soft under gentle hand pressure.

When opened, guavas contain scores of tiny, hard seeds that make eating the fruits difficult.

To prepare: With a sharp paring knife, peel off the skin, cut in half, remove and discard the seeds, and dice the fruit. To access the tropical sweetness of guava without the chore, use guava nectar or guava paste. Guava nectar is widely available and can be found in most supermarkets. Ceres (in a carton) and Kerns (in a can) put out great nectars. Guava paste is a thick, translucent jelly sold in tins. It has an incredibly long shelf life and is found in local Latin markets.

HIBISCUS

When the dried petals and calyxes from this tropical flower are brewed to make teas and coolers, they produce a liquid with a glorious red hue. Hibiscus has a pleasant, tangy, citruslike flavor and properties that sweeten the stomach and breath. The best hibiscus for brewing is the Jamaican *Hibiscus sabdariffa*, often marketed as red zinger. The fresh petals or flowers make a colorful, edible garnish.

To prepare: The only preparation needed for the fresh flowers is a gentle washing.

KIWIFRUIT

Also known as the Chinese gooseberry, this unusual-looking egg-shaped fruit has brown, fuzzy skin and radiant green flesh speckled with hundreds of tiny, edible black seeds. The flavor is sweet at the outset but with a tart bite at the finish. Choose one that is plump, heavy, and tender when gently squeezed. Available year-round, a single kiwi fruit contains as much vitamin C as four oranges.

To prepare: Pare away the peel and slice the flesh crosswise to reveal the attractive center for a garnish, or simply dice to use in blended drinks.

KUMQUAT

A tiny, grape-sized orange citrus fruit, the aromatic kumquat is extraordinarily tart and bitter unless eaten when very, very ripe. It can be consumed whole, for the rind is thin and tender, but as a drink ingredient, its flavor is best utilized in the form of a syrup. The zest of the rind is more often used than the flesh, although the most common way to consume this exotic Asian fruit is candied whole or pickled. The slightly larger, rounder variety from Florida is a sweeter choice.

To prepare: Peel the thin skin from the fruit, and cut the skin into thin strips. Twist the peels to release the aromatic oils, and drop into your favorite iced tea. Or cut in half with a sharp knife and add a few to a batch of simple syrup (see page 27).

LEMON

Choose a heavy lemon with a thin skin. The rind of a lemon holds aromatic oils that are released when a peel is twisted and dropped into a drink, adding an acidic tang. Lemons are available year-round, and fresh lemon juice is the ideal ingredient, but bottled lemon juice or frozen concentrate can be substituted in some recipes. The Meyer lemon, a sweet variety with a thin, smooth skin and particularly fragrant and juicy flesh, is common in warmer climes.

To prepare: Applying pressure with the palm of your hand, roll the lemon back and forth against a cutting board. This will soften the rind and loosen the juices for easier juicing. Slice in half and squeeze out the juice by hand or with an electric juicer.

LIME

The most common variety is the dark green Persian lime. Specialty food markets usually sell a second variety, the Key lime. Grown primarily in Florida, it has a yellowish green rind, is smaller, and has far more seeds than the Persian. Available irregularly throughout the year, Key limes are acidic with a touch of sweetness. Look for limes that yield to the touch and have a thin skin. Avoid hard limes, as they are past juicing.

Frozen limeade is a fine alternative in many recipes, especially if you are looking for the added bonus of sweetness. Lime juice and Key lime juice, both sold in bottles without additives or sugars, are found in most supermarkets. The aromatic oils from the lime rind form an integral part of the caipirinha.

To prepare: Use the directions for lemons (above).

LYCHEE

Native to China, the lychee (also spelled litchi) is juicy and sweet when ripe. The reddish brown shell is leathery and thin, while the translucent white flesh is fragrantly perfumed; tastes like a sweet, rosy grape, and has a single brown seed at its heart. In season from May through July, fresh lychees are difficult to find in supermarkets here, although Asian stores regularly carry them. The juice or nectar, tea, and even canned whole fruits are available at Asian markets as well. To store the fresh fruits, wrap them in paper towels, slip into a perforated plastic bag, and refrigerate for up to two weeks

To prepare: Peel and remove the brown seed.

MANGO

This sweet and fragrant fruit has an intoxicating liqueurlike flavor. There are many different varieties to choose from, all with their own distinct taste. Look for fruit with unblemished skin and no soft spots. Ripe mango is aromatic and slightly soft when squeezed, and will vary in color from yellow to orange or red skin. If you purchase a green fruit, let it ripen in a paper bag at room temperature. Once ripened, it can be refrigerated for a few days, or diced or pureed and frozen for several months. In addition to the fresh fruits, mango juice and diced and frozen mango flesh are sold in many markets.

To prepare: Preparing a mango can be a messy business but well worth it. With a sharp knife, pare off the skin. Then, standing the mango on its long, narrow side, carve off the flesh lengthwise in a single piece, getting as close as you can to the long, flat seed at the center.

MINT

Bunches of fresh mint sprigs are typically available in supermarket produce sections, especially peppermint and spearmint, although other intriguing types, from lemon to pineapple to apple, can sometimes be found.

To prepare: To release their sweet, cooling properties, muddle the leaves or mix with other ingredients in blended drinks and brewed teas.

ORANGE AND TANGERINE

When choosing an orange, opt for a fruit that is firm and heavy for its size. Avoid fruit that feels spongy when squeezed. Color is not an indication of ripeness. A wide selection of orange juice is available, from frozen concentrate to juice from a carton to fresh-squeezed.

Two additional members of the orange family turn up in tropical drinks, the blood orange and the tangerine or mandarin orange. Easy to spot with its red or purplish flesh and red-tinted orange rind, the once rare blood orange now enjoys considerable popularity. It has a sweet flavor that boasts subtle hints of berry flavor. The tangerine typically has a slightly more acidic, tart flavor than an orange, although some varieties can be quite sweet. While the name *tangerine* is common in the United States, the Europeans call this fruit a mandarin, indicating its true birthplace, China.

To prepare: Cut the fruit in half and squeeze by hand or with an electric juicer. Seedless varieties are preferable for drink recipes.

PAPAYA

This pear-shaped fruit is tender to the touch, has golden yellow skin and orange-pink flesh, is loaded with black seeds, and boasts an exotic sweet-tart flavor. The Solo is the most common variety available, although the sweeter, more flavorful Strawberry papaya from Hawaii is highly recommended. Papayas are available year-round, but the juice or nectar, stocked in many supermarkets, makes a terrific substitute for the fresh fruit.

To prepare: Pare off the skin, halve, and remove and discard the seeds. Cut the flesh as directed for drink preparation. Diced and frozen papaya is a wonderful addition to any blended tropical drink.

PASSION FRUIT

The type of passion fruit most commonly found in the United States is shaped like a small lemon. When ripe, it boasts rich purple or bright yellow skin, feels heavy for its size, is slightly deflated looking, and when the fruit is shaken, the juice within is audible. The inedible outer rind is leathery and wrinkled, while the interior reveals a bright orange flesh bearing hundreds of tiny, black edible seeds. The perfumed flavor of the passion fruit has a honey sweetness along with tart lime tones. Each fruit yields only a tablespoon or two of usable pulp. Passion-fruit juice or nectar is the most useful form for preparing drink recipes. Frozen passion-fruit puree can be found at Latin markets.

To prepare: Holding the fruit over a bowl, slice it in half crosswise. Scoop out the fleshy pulp with the black seeds. Place the pulp into ice-cube trays and freeze, or add to a drink straightaway. If you don't like the seeds, strain the pulp through a fine-mesh metal strainer and then use or freeze.

PINEAPPLE

Named for its resemblance to a pinecone, the pineapple is readily available year-round. When choosing a fresh pineapple at the store, turn the fruit upside down and smell the root end. If it is ripe, it will have an obvious pineappley-sweet smell. The green diamond-patterned skin should be turning orange and yellow. Avoid any fruits that seem exceedingly hard or bruised with dark spots. Once cut, the fruit will have a tangy, sweet yet acidic flavor. The juice is conveniently available in a frozen concentrate or canned, both perfect for making drinks.

To prepare: Slice off the leafy top and the root end. Stand the fruit on one end and cut the rind off the fruit in long strips, conserving as much of the juicy yellow flesh as possible. Cut off the flesh close to the hard core, removing it in quarters lengthwise. Cut into cubes and toss in the blender for a fab frappé, or freeze for later use.

POMEGRANATE

The pomegranate has smooth, leathery red skin and a multi-chambered interior that contains tiny seeds, each surrounded by juicy red pulp that is sweet and tart at the same time.

Pomegranate juice is the basis for true grenadine syrup. Some products on the market are labeled grenadine but are nothing more than colored corn syrup, so make sure that you are buying the real thing. If you find this a tedious fruit to juice, buy unsweetened pomegranate juice and syrup in Asian markets and natural-foods stores.

To prepare: Slice the fruit into quarters. With a spoon, detach the seeds from the skin, pith, and membrane. Remove the seeds, enclose them in a piece of cheesecloth, and squeeze firmly with your hands. Keep in mind that the pomegranate juice will stain your hands red. One pomegranate yields approximately 1/4 cup juice.

RASPBERRY

Red or gold, deliciously sweet and with tiny edible seeds, raspberries, fresh or frozen, are a great addition to drinks. They are in season from May to October, but hothouse harvests can be found in the produce section at other times of the year as well.

To prepare: Simply rinse and add to your favorite blended drink. Frozen, they can be an eye-catching replacement for ice cubes.

STAR FRUIT

More commonly known outside the United States as a carambola, the star fruit received its name from the starlike shape that results when the fruit is sliced. Ripe star fruits are yellow or orange with a few blemishes along the ridges, are highly fragrant and juicy, and carry a flavor that ranges from a tangy sweetness to a lemon tartness. If only unripe green fruits are available at the market, take them home and let ripen at room temperature. The aesthetically pleasing fruit makes lovely garnishes (see page 21).

To prepare: Lay the fruit on its side and cut crosswise. The entire fruit is edible. It contains only a few seeds, which are best discarded.

TAMARIND

Packed with vitamin C, the fruit of the tamarind tree is a fuzzy brown seedpod about four inches long and containing a sour pulp covering good-sized seeds. Used throughout the Caribbean in drinks and sauces, its flavor falls somewhere between lime juice and prunes. You can purchase tamarind as canned juice, puree, or pulp in Latin markets. Indian stores sell a jarred, intensely flavored tamarind concentrate that is quickly diluted in hot water.

To prepare: To make tamarind liquid from packaged pulp, soak the pulp in boiling water for several minutes, occasionally mashing the pulp with the back of a spoon to break apart the fibers. Strain through a fine-mesh strainer to remove the fibers and seeds. Use a walnut-sized ball of pulp for each 1/2 cup boiling water.

UGLI FRUIT

This yellowish green citrus fruit is the size of a grapefruit and has a more wrinkled skin. Look for heavy fruit that yields to the touch but is still firm. The flavor is a cross between a sweet mandarin and a tart grapefruit. Extremely juicy, the ugli is a good substitute for either grapefruit or orange juice. Store in the refrigerator for no more than two weeks.

To prepare: Cut in half and squeeze out the juice by hand or use a reamer or electric juicer. One fruit yields about 1 1/2 to 2 cups juice.

WATERMELON

Cool, sweet, and refreshing, the watermelon is a celebrated addition to any summer picnic. Due to its thirst-quenching qualities, it is frequently used as an ingredient in Latin batidos. Watermelons can be checked for ripeness by thumping on the rind with an open hand. If the resounding noise is hollow, the melon is ripe. Never choose a watermelon that is bruised or has any flat sides, and store in a cool, dry place. Once cut open, a watermelon should be wrapped tightly, refrigerated, and used within a few days.

To prepare: Slice the watermelon in half and cut into wedges or cubes, removing the seeds before adding the pink flesh to your concoction. The cubes can be frozen as is, or they can be pureed in a blender and poured into an ice-cube tray to freeze, then used in blender drinks or in place of ice cubes in a summer cooler.

GARNISHES

If there's one thing steamy-weather drinks are known for, it's their infamously flashy garnishes—creations that revel in the celebration of the ornamental. The contemporary tropical cocktail may have moments of sleek minimalism when it aspires to the urbane, but eventually it cannot deny its exuberant roots. Whichever aesthetic path you choose, be it a single floating rose petal in a Tikitini, or a jam-packed shish kebab of flora and plastic fauna on a Honolulu Lulu, your garnish will decorate your drink with style.

BANANA SLICES

Slice crosswise at a slight angle. If you like, leave the yellow, unblemished peel on for color. Always cut the slices as close to serving as possible and, to prevent discoloration, dip them in lemon juice.

Gilding the Lily

Tropical cocktails give you an open invitation to embellish and festoon, to be creative and whimsical, artistic and romantic. A frosty chilled glass rimmed with a dusting of sweet cocoa, sea salt with citrus zest, or jewel-like turbinado sugar adds a fabulous flavor dimension and visual intrigue to any cocktail. An orchid floating in the cocktail sea or a beautifully arranged skewer of fresh fruit balanced on the rim of a glass creates elegance with the utmost simplicity. A single citrus spiral winding through a crystal-clear martini fans the desire to sip away blissfully. This hands-on guide to cocktail styling covers all the essentials, from how to fashion a kiwifruit slice and a palm-tree twist to how to make fancy coconut rims.

CITRUS GARNISHES

Since many drinks are citrus-based (lemon, lime, or orange), it's not surprising that a citrus garnish is frequently used as a natural complement. Choose unblemished citrus fruits and wash well before preparing. When cutting citrus peel for twists, spirals, or zest, avoid as much of the bitter white pith as possible as you remove the peel.

Spiral: The easiest way to remove a peel in a single long, narrow strip is with a vegetable peeler or canelle knife. Starting at one end of the fruit, pare off the peel in a continuous strip, slowly working your way around the fruit. Twist the strip around your finger, and then slowly drop it into the drink, where it will fall in an attractive spiral.

Twist: With a sharp paring knife or a vegetable peeler, remove 2-inch-long lengthwise strips of peel from the citrus fruit. Holding a strip color-side down over a drink, twist it to release the aromatic oils in the peel, then drop the strip into the drink.

Wheel or slice: Cut off both ends from the fruit. Place the fruit on its side and cut into slices $1/4$- to $1/2$-inch thick. To balance the wheel on a glass rim, starting from the edge, make a cut to the center. Or, leave the slice uncut and float it in the drink.

Zest: With a fine-holed grater or a zester remove the zest (the colored portion of the shiny outer peel). Use the grated or finely shredded zest to infuse syrups and teas, to coat glass rims, or for sprinkling over cream-topped hot drinks.

COCONUT

Coconut meat can be used in various ways to garnish a drink. First, cut off the brown skin with a paring knife, then grate with a fine-toothed grater or pare off paper-thin slices of the flesh of the coconut, and sprinkle on top of drinks. Alternately, cut the flesh (including the brown skin) into $1/4$-inch-wide segments with a sharp paring knife, then make a partial cut into the slice so that it can be balanced on the rim. Or, add a wedge of coconut to a skewer of fruits.

Coconut cups: Sometimes you have to go all out, island style, and give that Tobago Coconut Flip a cup befitting of its contents—a coconut-shell cup. For the best—and easiest—way to arrive at

hollowed-out coconut halves, look for "easy crack" coconuts and drain and halve as directed on page 13. For easy-prep cups, place the coconut halves into an oven preheated to 350 degrees F for 10 to 15 minutes. The flesh will shrink from the shell, making it easier to pry off.

FLOWERS

Pesticide-free edible flowers, such as orchid, violet, borage, rose, orange blossom, and hibiscus, add an exotic island touch to any tropical drink. Gently rinse the flower or petals and float on the top of the cocktail, or skewer with a cocktail pick and balance on the glass rim. You can also decorate a drink with a larger orchid or hibiscus by attaching it to the stem of a glass with a length of florist wire.

KIWIFRUIT SLICES

Cut the kiwifruit crosswise into $1/4$- to $1/2$-inch-thick slices, to display the intricate beauty of the pale green flesh. To balance a slice on the rim of a glass, cut a slit into the center of the slice.

KUMQUAT FLOWERS

This small member of the large citrus family adds an aromatic and attractive ornament to fizzy citrus-based drinks. To make a festive kumquat "flower," using a sharp paring knife, and starting at one end, cut 3 or 4 sections of the peel away from the fruit at regular intervals, leaving the sections attached at the opposite end. Curl the sections back like petals, to make an elegant and exotic garnish. Skewer a few kumquat flowers on a cocktail pick and balance the pick on the rim of a glass.

MELON

Melon garnishes can add a sculptural element to the rim of your favorite Midori (melon liqueur) cocktail. Cut the watermelon, with its dark green rind, or the cool green of a honeydew, into wedges or slices 1-inch-wide by 2- to 3-inches-long. Cut a 1-inch slit into the wedge and balance it on the rim of a glass. To make a colorful assemblage of balls, use a melon scoop to remove spheres from cantaloupe, honeydew, and watermelon, spear them onto a wooden skewer or cocktail pick, and balance on the rim of a glass.

PINEAPPLE

In the realm of garnishes, the pineapple is a versatile fruit, as it can be used from top to bottom. Incorporate the spiny leaves as a green accent with other colorful fruit garnishes. Lay the pineapple on its side and cut crosswise into $1/2$-inch-thick slices to create pineapple wheels with the rind intact for color and visual texture. Or, quarter the slices for smaller pineapple wedges.

Pineapple shell: For a fabulous, festive cup for a dreamy rum punch, cut off the spiny top of a pineapple and, using a sharp knife and spoon, scoop out the flesh, leaving the shell intact. Refrigerate until ready to use. Save the fruit and juice as a base for future drinks.

SOUTH SEAS SOUVENIRS

Tropical cocktails are festive by definition, and there are endless ways to set the mood, from the ornamental paper umbrella to the jungle-in-a-glass complete with hanging plastic monkeys. If you have been looking for an excuse to use those kitschy drink accessories, now is your chance. A floating plastic swordfish in a martini or a mermaid poised on the edge of a green elixir will liven up even the most serious cocktail.

STAR-FRUIT SLICES

To create an eye-catching star-shaped garnish, cut the star fruit crosswise into slices $1/4$- to $1/2$-inch thick. To balance a slice on the rim of a glass, cut a slit into the center of the slice. Or, leave the slice uncut and float it in the drink.

PACIFIC RIMS

Rim a glass with a dusting of something sweet or tart, textural and colorful, and you add visual appeal, elegance, and multidimensional flavor. The basic method can be applied to a variety of ingredients. Ideally, the glass will be chilled, but an unchilled glass will work in a pinch.

Basic Method

1. Pour 5 or 6 tablespoons of an ingredient (such as salt or sugar) on a small plate or in a small wide bowl and shake gently to distribute evenly. The amount will cover 3 or 4 rims.

2. Rub a lemon or lime wedge once around the rim of the glass to moisten it.

3. Turn the glass upside down and set the rim in the ingredient. Gently turn the glass back and forth to coat the rim completely, then shake off any excess.

4. Pour in your cocktail, being careful not to disturb the coated rim.

SALT RIM

Following the basic method, moisten the rim with lime juice and coat with sea salt.

SUGAR RIM

Moisten the rim with a citrus wedge and coat with superfine sugar. Turbinado sugar can give a bejeweled texture, perfect for chocolate- or coffee-based cocktails. For a delicate touch, use powdered sugar.

SALT AND SUGAR RIM

For a sweet-and-sour combination follow the basic method, moisten the rim with a lime wedge and coat with a mixture of equal amounts of sea salt and granulated sugar.

CITRUS ZEST RIM

A rim of salt and lime zest enhances the usual salt-only margarita, and a rim of orange, lemon, or lime zest mixed with sugar gives a flavor boost to a citrus-based cocktail. Moisten the rim of the glass with a complementary citrus wedge. Then coat the rim with a mixture of $1/4$ cup granulated sugar or sea salt and 3 tablespoons finely grated orange, lemon, or lime zest according to the basic method. Depending on the size of the glass, the mixture will cover 3 or 4 rims.

COCONUT RIM

For a festively tropical touch, dip the rim into a wide, shallow bowl filled with $1/4$ cup complementary liqueur such as Cointreau or Chambord, then coat with coconut according to the basic method. One-half cup coconut flakes or grated fresh coconut will coat 3 or 4 glass rims.

GRATED CHOCOLATE OR COCOA RIM

A chocolate rim complements drinks with lemon or orange flavors, or adds sweetness to coffee-based cocktails. A cocoa-coated rim is a fine addition to cream or ice-cream drinks. Following the basic method, moisten the rim with a citrus wedge, then coat with cocoa powder or grated chocolate. A few tablespoons of cocoa powder or $1/2$ cup grated chocolate will coat several glasses.

Rum Baby Rum

Rum is, literally and figuratively, the spirit of the Caribbean. Unlike other bottled spirits, it has a magical quality that, with just one sip, transports even the snowbound to a balmy, breezy, palm-festooned paradise. Whether enjoyed simply over ice or in your favorite daiquiri, rum is the quintessential element for the pure tropical flavor experience.

The lovely sweetness inherent in rum comes from sugarcane. It is pressed to extract the fresh juice, which is boiled down to a thick syrup. There are a few varieties of rum that are distilled from this pure sugarcane syrup, but most are derived from molasses, a by-product of sugar production. The sugar in the syrup is crystallized and removed through centrifugal force, and the remaining molasses is then fermented and distilled.

Rum can, of course, be produced wherever there is sugarcane, but the Caribbean is the heart and soul of the industry. Each island has its own distinctly different and perfected style, from the swarthy dark rums of Jamaica, Barbados, Trinidad, and Martinique to the silver, white, and other light rums of Cuba, Haiti, Puerto Rico, and the Virgin Islands. Although a relatively small number of Caribbean rums are imported to the United States (all the more reason to head out on a rum-tasting expedition), the selection is still varied.

In the wide world of rums, there are many nuances involved that overlap from one type to another, making the lines of classification somewhat blurry. With that in mind, the following guide offers the basic categories with insight into the types available.

LIGHT RUMS

Labeled either light, white, silver, or blanco, these rums are clear to pale gold, light bodied, and faintly sweet. Aged no longer than one year in uncharred white oak barrels or stainless-steel tanks, and usually filtered through charcoal for smoothness, their flavors range from floral and fruity (Cuban Havana Club) to neutral and crisp (Puerto Rican Bacardi) to soft and mellow with light coconut tones (Jamaican Appleton Estate). Because of its delicate flavor, light rum is an excellent choice for most frosty cocktails, from tall coolers to daiquiris.

GOLD RUMS

Labeled as gold (oro) or amber (ambre), these are smooth light rums turned golden through aging (typically one to three years) in charred barrels, and occasionally the color is adjusted with additional caramel coloring. They are used in many cocktails that call for light rum to add a slightly more intense flavor. One of the oldest Caribbean producers, Mount Cay on Barbados, puts out a fine gold rum, as does Jamaican Appleton Estate or my personal favorite, Barbancourt rum from Haiti.

DARK RUMS

Dark rums are made in traditional pot stills and aged anywhere from three to twelve years in well-charred oak barrels. The dark, heavy rums such as Myers's from Jamaica or those from Guyana add aggressive flavor to cocktails and are best used to enhance the lighter rums in the potent drinks. A splash of dark rum can deliver rich molasses flavor to tall, fruity cocktails. And for real dark-rum fans, the traditional Jamaican cocktail, Dark and Stormy, is made with Gosling's black rum and ginger beer. Excellent dark rums include Myers's Legend from Jamaica, a dark reserve blend with clove, cardamom, molasses, and coffee flavors and those bottled by Demerara distillers in Guyana.

AGED RUMS

Similar in quality to a good brandy or bourbon, these brown rums, which are also known as *rhum vieux* (usually bottled in France and aged at least three years) or *añejo* (aged Spanish rums that have no set minimum), are to be enjoyed like Cognac. Unlike most dark rums, which are heavily flavored, these spirits draw their intensity from a longer aging period and are always more expensive than their younger counterparts. Most aged rums are blended, but connoisseurs seek out single-mark rums, that is, rums drawn from a single batch. These are rare and very expensive.

A few aged blends are worth trying whenever you mix up a batch of (very dry) rum martinis. Bacardi 8 is an eight-year-old blend, with intonations of orange blossom, pears, apples, and caramel. Gran Blason Añejo Especial, from Costa Rica, has a slightly smoky flavor and a

coffeelike bitterness. The French West Indies are known for producing some of the finest rhum vieux, so if you can find a way to Martinique, don't miss the opportunity to sample one; the Saint James is sublime.

SPICED AND FLAVORED RUMS

Growing in popularity, spiced and flavored rums come infused with the flavor of citrus, vanilla, coconut, pineapple, or various other fruits and spices. Sold as rum liqueurs, bottled rum punches, and rum infusions, they give an additional flavor kick to many cocktails. Of course, the traditional favorite is Captain Morgan Spiced Rum from Puerto Rico, great for hot rum drinks and spiced-up rum punch.

OVERPROOF RUMS

The overproof rums, like Bacardi 151 or Demerara, are harsh, potent, and flammable and not for drinking straight, by any means. These notorious spirits are used to raise the alcohol content of "only two-per-customer" Zombie-inspired concoctions, and as the theatrical element in flaming drinks and desserts.

THE OTHER RUM: CACHAÇA

A distant cousin to rum, cachaça is also made from sugarcane, but while rum is made from molasses, cachaça is made from the juice of the first press of unrefined sugarcane. It has a fiery tone, harsher than rum, and a bite similar to brandy. This is Brazil's national liquor, with four thousand different brands from which to choose. Luckily, a few, such as Cachaça 51 and Toucano by Ypioca, have made their way into the United States.

Agave Enlightenment

Tequila has come a long way from its old image of harsh, macho firewater tossed back in shots. A whole new stratum of deluxe tequilas has risen to a refined level of snifter-quality smoothness. No longer considered south-of-the-border cactus water, tequila has become the drink of the hip and savvy spirit connoisseurs who demand tequila Cosmopolitans and Cadillac margaritas.

Produced primarily in the state of Jalisco, Mexico, tequila is made from the huge heart, or *piña*, of the blue agave plant. The best-quality tequilas will say "100 percent blue agave" on the label, signifying they have superior flavor, were bottled in Mexico, and were produced with sugar that was all from the blue agave and not a blend of different sugars. These pure agave tequilas are the only way to go. You may be tempted to pick up a cheaper brand when your guests are demanding yet another pitcher of margaritas, but a sublime cocktail versus the ordinary and predictable is well worth the expense.

Tequilas have varying degrees of quality and flavor, from harsh, rough blends to smooth añejos. The following Agave 101 guide will help you decipher the information on the labels of all those tempting tequilas on the market.

SILVER TEQUILAS

The silver (plata) or white (blanco) tequilas are freshly distilled and bottled within 60 days. Although these clear spirits have a fiery quality, making them a bit harsher than the aged tequilas, their full-on flavor is perfect for fruity margaritas and spicy concoctions.

GOLD TEQUILAS

Gold refers to the caramel color, as these are not aged tequilas, but rather silver tequilas with added coloring and flavoring that slightly mellows them out. Also known as *dorado* tequilas, the golds are well suited to shots and shooters.

REPOSADO TEQUILAS

"Rested" tequilas, mellowed and improved by aging two months to a year in oak barrels, are very smooth. The pale gold to deeper gold hues come from aging, although sometimes additional coloring has been added as well. Chinaco reposado is a personal favorite. Traces of honey and vanilla tones add a rich, warm dimension to margaritas. Reposados also warrant straight sipping.

AÑEJO TEQUILAS

Meaning "aged," the name says it all. These deluxe tequilas are aged at least one year, and no more than five, in wood barrels. Typically made with 100 percent agave, they are highly regulated for quality and are label dated. Some coloring and flavoring are permitted. The best añejos are a perfect taste balance of tequila and wood, versus those that weigh in with a predominantly heavy wood flavor. These aged tequilas are the sip-able equivalent of a good Cognac.

Jungle Juice

When it comes to mixing a superb drink, good-quality ingredients are essential. Some flavored syrups and infused spirits are readily available in stores, but when you make your own, the flavor you gain is worth the effort. Infusing syrups and spirits with the essence of a fruit, spice, or herb is surprisingly easy and opens up a sea of possibilities for more flavor adventures.

SYRUPS

Homemade syrups are a convenient and quick way to add the essence of a fruit or a spice to a drink, as they blend with ease in mixed drinks. They can be made ahead of time and stored in the refrigerator, where they will keep for up to two weeks.

SIMPLE SYRUP

Easily made (hence its name), this recipe is the base for a multitude of differently flavored syrups and will keep for up to a month in the refrigerator.

1 cup water

2 cups sugar

1. In a small saucepan, bring the water to a boil. Add the sugar and stir slowly until dissolved. Reduce the heat to low and let simmer for 5 minutes.

2. Remove from the heat and let cool completely, about 30 minutes.

3. Pour into a clean glass jar, cap tightly, and store in the refrigerator.

Makes 2 cups

FLAVORED SYRUPS

The following flavored syrup variations start with the simple syrup recipe. Add the flavorings once the sugar has completely dissolved and the syrup has just reached the simmering stage. When the syrup has cooled, strain it through a fine-mesh metal strainer for storage.

Ginger Syrup: Add 2 tablespoons finely grated fresh ginger to the simmering syrup. Remove from the heat, let cool, strain, cap, and refrigerate.

Hibiscus Syrup: Use strongly steeped hibiscus tea in place of the water and proceed according to the directions for simple syrup.

Kumquat Syrup: Add 10 small kumquats, sliced in half, to the simmering syrup. Remove from the heat and allow the kumquats to continue to infuse the syrup for 45 minutes while the syrup cools. Strain, reserving the kumquats, cap, and refrigerate. Save the poached kumquats in another container and freeze to use as flavored "ice cubes" in the Shanghai Sling (see page 71).

Lemongrass Syrup: Add 2 fresh lemongrass stalks, cut into 1/2-inch pieces, to the simmering syrup. Remove from the heat and allow the lemongrass to continue to infuse the syrup for 45 minutes while the syrup cools. Strain, cap, and refrigerate.

Mint Syrup: Add 1/2 cup fresh spearmint leaves to the simmering syrup. Remove from the heat, let cool, strain, cap, and refrigerate.

SWEET AND SOUR

This is one of my favorite cut-to-the-chase ingredients. Covering both the sweet and the citrus factors at the same time, it is handy to have on hand. There's no comparison between the store-bought mix and the marvelous quality this freshly made concoction provides. This recipe yields enough for about 10 drinks.

1 cup cooled simple syrup (see page 27)
³/₄ cup fresh lime juice
³/₄ cup fresh lemon juice

1. Combine the syrup, lime juice, and lemon juice in a clean glass jar. Cap tightly and shake the contents until well mixed.

2. Refrigerate until needed. This syrup will keep for up to 10 days.

Makes 2 ¹/₂ cups

TROPICAL INFUSIONS

Infused liquors are the new, creative expression in the world of serious mixology. Vodka is the ideal blank canvas for infusing with a Gauguin-like intensity of island spices. But you can also take rum to the next level of exotica using tropical fruits, or give tequila an additional fiery bite with hot chiles. Infusions are surprisingly easy to make, and the end result adds wonderful depth of flavor to any spirit. To dispel any infusion confusion, here are a few guidelines:

1. Use a clean, large 1 ¹/₂-quart glass container with an airtight lid.

2. Start with 1 liter good-quality liquor, and use fresh ripe fruits, spices, or herbs.

3. Save your original bottle, as you will need to strain the infused mixture into it.

4. Infusion times vary, depending on the ingredient. Strong flavors like lemon take less time to steep (24 to 48 hours), while milder flavors such as raspberries or pineapple may take from 1 to 3 weeks to infuse sufficiently.

5. Some ingredients may break down to the point that the spirit will need to be strained through a fine-mesh metal strainer lined with cheesecloth or a coffee filter.

6. Infusions are best stored in the refrigerator, as chilling helps preserve the flavors longer.

RUM INFUSIONS

These rummy infusions take you directly into the tropical zone. Sip them straight to enjoy the fine flavor nuances, or give your basic daiquiri or punch a luscious complexity. The infused spirits will keep indefinitely when stored in the refrigerator.

Coconut Rum

3 cups freshly grated coconut
1 liter good-quality light rum

1. Place the coconut in the glass container, add the rum, and cap tightly.

2. Let stand at room temperature for 3 weeks, shaking the container gently every couple of days.

3. Taste for the preferred flavor intensity, allowing it to infuse for up to 1 week longer if it needs more time.

4. Using a funnel and a fine-mesh wire strainer, strain the mixture into the original rum bottle. Cap tightly, label, and refrigerate until servng.

Vanilla Rum

4 vanilla beans, broken into small pieces

1 liter good-quality silver or gold rum

1. Add the vanilla bean pieces to the bottle of rum and cap tightly.

2. Let stand at room temperature for at least 1 week, shaking the bottle gently every couple of days.

3. Refrigerate to infuse the rum indefinitely. When ready to use, slowly strain the vanilla-infused rum through a fine-mesh metal strainer into the jigger or glass.

Pineapple Rum

1 pineapple, peeled, cored, and cut into small cubes

1 liter good-quality light rum

1. Place the pineapple cubes in the glass container, add the rum, and cap tightly.

2. Let stand at room temperature for 1 week, shaking the container gently every couple of days.

3. Transfer the mixture to the refrigerator and allow it to infuse for another week, shaking the container gently every couple of days. Taste for the preferred flavor intensity, allowing it to infuse for up to 1 week longer if it needs more time.

4. Using a funnel and a fine-mesh wire strainer, strain the mixture into the original rum bottle. Cap tightly, label, and refrigerate until serving.

VODKA INFUSIONS

There are a variety of ways to create an intriguing and innovative vodka martini. Following the method for ginger vodka, try infusing a liter of vodka with 2 cups fresh mint leaves; $1/2$ cup fresh rosemary leaves; 2 vanilla beans, broken into pieces; or the peel from 1 large lemon, orange, tangerine, or lime. Infused vodka will keep indefinitely when stored in the refrigerator.

Ginger Vodka

1 cup thinly sliced fresh ginger

1 liter good-quality vodka

1. Place the ginger in the glass container, add the vodka, and cap tightly.

2. Let stand at room temperature for 2 days, shaking the container gently every so often.

3. Taste for the preferred flavor intensity, allowing it to infuse for up to 4 days longer if it needs more time.

4. Using a funnel and a fine-mesh metal strainer, strain the mixture back into the original vodka bottle. Cap tightly, label, and refrigerate until serving.

Watermelon Vodka

3 cups cubed watermelon
1 liter good-quality vodka

1. *Place the watermelon in the glass container, add the vodka, and cap tightly.*

2. *Let stand at room temperature for 1 week, shaking the container gently every few days.*

3. *Taste for the preferred flavor intensity, allowing it to infuse for up to 4 days longer if it needs more time. Do not allow it to infuse any longer, or a bitter flavor will result.*

4. *Using a funnel and a fine-mesh metal strainer lined with cheesecloth, strain the mixture back into the original vodka bottle. Cap tightly, label, and refrigerate until serving.*

TEQUILA INFUSIONS

This pair of tequila infusions, one laced with spicy chiles (perfect for those bloody margaritas) and the other with fragrant vanilla, will fuel any cocktail with complex flavor. They will keep indefinitely in the refrigerator.

Vanilla Tequila

4 vanilla beans, broken into small pieces
1 liter good-quality silver tequila

1. *Add the vanilla bean pieces to the bottle of tequila and cap tightly.*

2. *Let stand at room temperature for at least 1 week, shaking the bottle gently every couple of days.*

3. *Refrigerate to infuse the tequila indefinitely. When ready to use, slowly strain the vanilla-infused tequila through a fine-mesh metal strainer into the jigger or glass.*

Pepper Tequila

1 serrano chile pepper, stemmed, quartered lengthwise, and seeded
1 jalapeño chile pepper, stemmed, quartered lengthwise, and seeded
1 red chile pepper, stemmed, quartered lengthwise, and seeded
1 bottle (750 ml) good-quality silver tequila

1. *Place all the peppers in the glass container, add the tequila, and cap tightly.*

2. *Let stand at room temperature for 2 days, shaking the container gently every so often.*

3. *Using a funnel and a fine-mesh metal strainer lined with cheesecloth, strain the tequila back into the original tequila bottle.*

4. *Cap tightly, label, and refrigerate until serving.*

CHAPTER 1

THE Tropitini

THE URBAN MARTINI GOES SOUTH AND DIVES RIGHT INTO A DAZZLING OCEAN OF FLAVOR. ALTHOUGH THE RESURGENCE OF THE COCKTAIL HAS FUELED COUNTLESS DEBATES ON WHAT EXACTLY CONSTITUTES A "TINI," AND SOME PURISTS STAND FIRMLY BEHIND THE DRY GIN VERSION, A LEGION OF NEWLY CREATED COCKTAILS DESIGNED AROUND PREMIUM LIQUORS AND FLAVOR-INFUSED SPIRITS HAS EVOLVED. TRANSLUCENT JEWEL-TONED ELIXIRS SHIMMERING IN STYLISH GLASSES HAVE BECOME DE RIGUEUR. LIKE ANY GOOD MARTINI, TROPITINIS ARE PERFECTLY PROPORTIONED AND UTTERLY REFINED. SMOOTH, LUXURIOUS, AND POTENT, THESE SEDUCTIVE SELECTIONS STRAIGHT FROM PARADISE ARE GUARANTEED TO SEDUCE EVEN THE MOST FANATICAL MISSIONARIES OF THE CLASSIC MARTINI.

BLUE MARLIN

TIKITINI

KEY LIME MARTINI

JAVANESE MARTINI

THE ROYAL PALM COCKTAIL

THE HOWELLS' MARTINI ("FOR LOVEY")

PEARL DIVER

BLUE MARLIN

Like an incoming tide, clear, turquoise-blue waters lap the sides of your cocktail glass, and the aromas of lemon and orange play on your senses. Under the influence of this tropical potion, you may even see visions of a diving blue marlin. More likely, you will have one of those flashy blue plastic cocktail fishes swimming in your drink. Whatever the case, you can thank the island of Curaçao for the aquamarine illusion produced by its intense blue liqueur, which imparts a sweet orange flavor to this deep sea concoction.

Lemon zest–sugar rim (see page 22)
1 1/2 cups cracked ice or 6 ice cubes
  2 ounces citron rum
 1/2 ounce blue curaçao
 1/2 ounce sweet and sour (see page 28)
  1 orange blossom for garnish

1. Coat the rim of a chilled cocktail glass with sugar and lemon zest. Chill until needed.

2. Fill a cocktail shaker with the ice and add the rum, curaçao, and sweet and sour. Shake vigorously to blend and chill.

3. Strain the mixture into the prepared glass, float the orange blossom on top and serve.

Serves 1

TIKITINI

The martini meets the *Kon Tiki* in this fruity ambrosia from the gods, rimmed with coconut of course. There's no holding back the exuberance of the tropical island flavors blooming in this cocktail. Once you sip the fine balance between the sweetness of the mango and pineapple and the bitter almond flavor of the maraschino liqueur, you'll feel an intense desire to shove a hibiscus behind one ear and walk barefoot into the surf.

Coconut rim (see page 22)
1 1/2 cups cracked ice or 6 ice cubes
2 1/2 ounces pineapple rum,
     (see page 29)
 1/2 ounce maraschino liqueur
 1/2 ounce coconut milk (see page 13)
  2 ounces mango juice
  1 small yellow orchid for garnish

1. Coat the rim of a chilled 6-ounce cocktail glass with coconut. Chill until needed.

2. Fill a cocktail shaker with the ice and add the rum, maraschino liqueur, coconut milk, and mango juice. Shake vigorously to blend and chill.

3. Strain the mixture into the prepared glass, float the flower on top, and serve.

Serves 1

KEY LIME MARTINI

For a taste that takes you straight to the Keys, just shake up one of these. This lime green elixir gets its pucker from the juice of Key limes and its sweet kick and gentle orange flavor from Harlequin liqueur. Key limes are yellow when mature and are smaller than the more common green Persian limes. This recipe requires 4 to 6 key limes or 2 or 3 Persian limes.

Superfine sugar rim (see page 22)

1½ cups cracked ice or 6 ice cubes

3 ounces good-quality gin

2 ounces Harlequin (orange liqueur)

3 ounces fresh Key lime or other lime juice

¼ cup superfine sugar

2 lime wheels (see page 20) for garnish

1. Coat the rims of 2 chilled cocktail glasses with sugar. Chill until needed.

2. Fill a cocktail shaker with the ice and add the gin, Harlequin, lime juice, and sugar. Shake vigorously to blend and chill.

3. Strain the mixture into the prepared glasses, dividing it evenly. Decorate each rim with a lime wheel and serve.

Serves 2

JAVANESE MARTINI

The secret to this dark, aromatic, spicy cocktail is to brew the espresso with a pinch of cinnamon added to the ground coffee. A tangy sweetness is provided by the rum-based Tia Maria, which is made from Jamaican Blue Mountain coffee. This energetic and spirited martini is intense enough to fuel a night of trance dancing under the volcano.

Turbinado sugar rim (see page 22)
1½ **cups cracked Ice or 6 ice cubes**
1½ **ounces good-quality vodka**
  1 **ounce espresso brewed with cinnamon, cooled**
  1 **ounce Tia Maria (coffee liqueur)**
  1 **lemon-peel twist (see page 20) for garnish**

1. Coat the rim of a chilled cocktail glass with turbinado sugar. Chill until needed.

2. Fill a cocktail shaker with the ice and add the vodka, espresso, and Tia Maria. Shake vigorously to blend and chill.

3. Strain the mixture into the prepared glass. Twist the lemon peel over the drink, drop it in, and serve.

Serves 1

THE ROYAL PALM COCKTAIL

Glasses tinkle and palm fronds rustle while shimmering in the moonlight. But it's the whisper of a sultry island beat that you hear as you sip vanilla-infused bliss with a trace of banana . . . 99 Bananas to be exact.

½ **ounce 99 Bananas liqueur or crème de banana**
1½ **cups cracked ice or 6 ice cubes**
  2 **ounces vanilla rum (see page 29)**
½ **vanilla bean for garnish**

1. Chill a cocktail glass.

2. Pour the banana liqueur into the chilled glass and swirl to coat the inside of the glass completely. Discard any excess liqueur.

3. Fill a cocktail shaker with the ice and add the vanilla rum. Shake vigorously to chill.

4. Strain the rum into the chilled glass. Garnish with the vanilla bean and serve.

Serves 1

THE HOWELLS' MARTINI ("FOR LOVEY")

Never at a loss when it came to the finer details of life, the Howells were castaways who knew how to be stranded with style. When it came to traveling, they had their priorities in order. These savvy adventurers would never think of embarking on a three-hour boat tour without their cocktail case, complete with shaker, glasses, and the finest gin. One might imagine their perfected deserted-isle martini to be a playful intertwining of the delicate juniper flavor of gin with a whisper of tropical passion fruit from Alizé de France, a Cognac-based liqueur blended with passion-fruit juice. Of course, *daahling*, one must talk through one's teeth while shaking up this island elixir.

- 1/2 **ounce Alizé de France (passion-fruit liqueur)**
- 1 1/2 **cups cracked ice or 6 ice cubes**
- 2 **ounces Bombay Sapphire gin**
- 1 **lemon-peel spiral (see page 19) for garnish**

1. *Chill a cocktail glass.*

2. *Pour the liqueur into the chilled glass and swirl around to coat the inside of the glass completely. Discard any excess liqueur.*

3. *Fill a cocktail shaker with the ice and add the gin. Shake vigorously to chill.*

4. *Strain the gin into the chilled glass. Drop in the lemon spiral, and serve.*

Serves 1

PEARL DIVER ▶

Dive for this pan-Asian pearl of a cocktail, as translucent as the South China Sea, and its pure modern minimalism: spicy ginger-infused vodka swirled with Momokawa Pearl sake.

- 1 1/2 **cups cracked ice or 6 ice cubes**
- 2 **ounces ginger vodka (see page 29)**
- 1/2 **ounce Momokawa Pearl or other premium sake, chilled**
- 1 **thin slice candied ginger for garnish**

1. *Chill a cocktail glass.*

2. *Fill a cocktail shaker with the ice and add the vodka. Shake vigorously to chill.*

3. *Strain the vodka into the chilled glass. Slowly pour in the sake, floating it on top of the vodka.*

4. *For the garnish, make a cut to the center of the candied ginger slice, balance the slice on the rim of the glass, and serve.*

Serves 1

CHAPTER 2

Eye of
THE HURRICANE

TIDAL WAVE

MONSOON OVER MIAMI

TASMANIAN TWISTER

VOLCANIC BLAST

BARRACUDA BREEZE

HONOLULU LULU

EQUATORIAL ELIXIRS THAT PACK A WALLOP

BATTEN DOWN THE LAMPSHADES AND HOIST UP THE CHANDELIERS. THESE ZOMBIE-INSPIRED HURRICANES-IN-A-GLASS WILL BLOW THE ROOF OFF ANY CIVILIZED GATHERING. THE COLLECTION OF FRUITY NECTARS, RICH RUMS, AND LUSCIOUS LIQUEURS COME TOGETHER IN A WHIRLWIND OF POWERFUL ELIXIRS THAT DEFY THE PREMISE THAT LESS IS MORE. SO PULL OUT YOUR MOST GARGANTUAN GLASSWARE AND FESTOON YOUR POTENT CONCOCTIONS WITH SKEWERS OF FRESH FRUIT AND FLOATING EXOTICA, LEAVING JUST ENOUGH ROOM FOR A FEW STRAWS.

TIDAL WAVE

This frothy aquamarine concoction will knock you right off your surfboard. Made with Malibu, the rum-based coconut-flavored liqueur from the Caribbean, and a splash of orange, lime, and almond flavors as big as a tsunami, it is sparky enough for even the most jaded beachnik to sip.

1½ **cups cracked ice or 6 ice cubes**
  3 **ounces Malibu rum**
  2 **ounces blue curaçao**
1½ **ounces fresh lime juice**
  1 **ounce amaretto**
  2 **tablespoons coconut cream (see page 13)**
  1 **tablespoon superfine sugar**
  2 **small purple orchids for garnish**

1. *Chill 2 cocktail glasses.*

2. *Fill a cocktail shaker with the ice and add the rum, curaçao, lime juice, amaretto, coconut cream, and sugar. Shake vigorously to blend and chill.*

3. *Strain the mixture into the chilled glasses, dividing it evenly. Garnish each drink with an orchid and serve.*

Serves 2

42

MONSOON OVER MIAMI

Although this cocktail has a breezy Southern refinement and goes down as smoothly as a mint julep, it packs a typhoonlike wallop. A whirl of quintessential summer flavors—watermelon and lemon citrus—is effervescently swept together with a splash of chilled Champagne. This South Beach–inspired brew is the perfect libation to serve at your next Sunday brunch.

   1 **cup cubed watermelon**
1 1/2 **ounces Absolut Citron or other lemon vodka**
   1/2 **ounce sweet and sour (see page 28)**
   6 **ice cubes**
1 or 2 **ounces Champagne, chilled**

GARNISH:
   1 **lemon-peel spiral (see page 19)**
   1 **watermelon wedge**

1. In a blender, combine the watermelon cubes, vodka, and sweet and sour. Blend until the watermelon is pureed and the ingredients are well combined.

2. Fill a tall 10-ounce glass with the ice and pour the mixture into the glass.

3. Top off with the Champagne. Drop in the lemon-peel spiral, place the watermelon wedge on the rim of the glass, and serve.

Serves 1

TASMANIAN TWISTER

A feisty island citrus lifts the urban Negroni cocktail into a whirlwind of palate-twisting flavors. Juicy ugli fruit hovers somewhere between sweet tangerine and tart grapefruit. If you have a difficult time finding this tropical citrus, pink grapefruit juice is an equally fabulous option. Shake up a few Twisters and sip to the intonations of some crazy Australian outback tune on the hi-fi.

1 1/2 **cups cracked ice or 6 ice cubes**
   1 **ounce good-quality gin**
   1 **ounce sweet vermouth**
   1 **ounce Campari**
   2 **ounces fresh ugli-fruit juice**
   1 **ugli fruit–peel or orange-peel twist (see page 20) for garnish**

1. Chill a large cocktail glass.

2. Fill a cocktail shaker with the ice and add the gin, sweet vermouth, Campari, and ugli-fruit juice. Shake vigorously to blend and chill.

3. Strain the mixture into the chilled glass. Run the ugli fruit–peel around the rim of the glass, twist, drop it into the drink, and serve.

Serves 1

VOLCANIC BLAST

Ignite your senses with this volatile cocktail shooter. Spicy rum is layered with the island flavors of mandarin orange, papaya, and Kahlúa. As the initial heady nature of the rum hits, you receive a blast of citrus, then the refreshing fruity tone of the papaya mingled with the sweet warmth of the coffee liqueur. The trick to keeping the colorful liquids in their strata is to pour each ingredient very slowly. Sip through all the layers of flavor to decipher their complexity, or shoot it straight and imagine the subtleties.

- ¼ **ounce Kahlúa**
- ¼ **ounce Mandarine Napoléon (mandarin liqueur)**
- ¼ **ounce raspberry syrup**
- ¼ **ounce papaya juice**
- ¼ **ounce Captain Morgan spiced rum**
- ½ **teaspoon 151-proof rum**

1. Pour the Kahlúa into a heatproof 2-ounce shot glass or pousse-café glass.

2. Continue to layer the ingredients: with the bowl inverted, angle a spoon into the glass, and slowly pour each liquid over the back of the spoon, in order—Mandarine Napoléon, raspberry syrup, papaya juice, spiced rum, 151-proof rum—and one at a time.

3. Using a long match, carefully ignite the 151-proof rum and let it burn for a few seconds. Blow out the flame and let the glass cool a bit before sipping.

Serves 1

BARRACUDA BREEZE ▶

This is one of those oh-so-innocent, pretty, pink drinks whose ultrasmoothness belies its mind-altering properties. Easy and breezy, this potent lemonade is spiked with a toothy tequila bite from Chinaco reposado (my favorite aged tequila) and is complemented by the zingy citrus tingle of lemoncello liqueur and a cooling splash of club soda. Served in a tall glass, this tropical equivalent of the vodka-based Sea Breeze is the perfect accompaniment for an afternoon picnic of grilled fish and succulent fruit.

- 4 **ounces reposado tequila**
- 1 **cup (8 ounces) guava nectar**
- 2 **ounces lemoncello (lemon liqueur)**
- 1½ **ounces fresh lemon juice**
- 1 **tablespoon superfine sugar**
- 10 to 12 **ice cubes**
- 2 to 4 **ounces club soda**
- 2 **lemon wedges for garnish**

1. In a blender, combine the tequila, guava nectar, lemoncello, lemon juice, and sugar. Blend until well combined.

2. Fill 2 tall 14-ounce glasses with the ice and divide the blended mixture evenly between the glasses.

3. Top off with the club soda and stir slowly to combine. Decorate the rim of each glass with a lemon wedge and serve.

Serves 2

HONOLULU LULU

Nutty about macadamias? This one is a lulu all right, and may just be the ambrosia that pushes your buttons into a high hula euphoria. A turbulent whirl of dark and nutty flavors with a zing of lime, this rhythmic concoction is based on the Hawaiian Islands manifesto that defines traditional rum punch. The sacrosanct rules are as follows: one part sour (citrus), two parts sweet (syrup or liqueur), three parts strong (rum), and four parts weak (juice).

Pineapple shell (see page 21)
1½ cups cracked ice or 6 ice cubes
1½ ounces Myers's dark rum
1 ounce light rum
1 ounce macadamia nut liqueur
½ ounce Kahlúa
4 ounces pineapple juice
1 ounce fresh lime juice
1 ounce hibiscus syrup (see page 27)

GARNISH:
1 lime wedge
1 hibiscus flower

1. *Prepare and chill a pineapple shell.*

2. *Fill a cocktail shaker with the ice and add the dark and light rums, macadamia nut liqueur, Kahlúa, pineapple juice, lime juice, and hibiscus syrup. Shake vigorously to blend and chill.*

3. *Take the top off the shaker and pour the mixture, ice and all, into the pineapple shell. Skewer the lime wedge and hibiscus flower together with a cocktail pick and decorate the rim of the shell. Serve with a straw.*

Serves 1

CHAPTER 3

Daiquirama

VARIATIONS ON A DAIQUIRI THEME

ACCORDING TO LEGEND, AROUND 1896, WHILE PARTYING IN THE CUBAN VILLAGE OF DAIQUIRI, JENNINGS COX, AN AMERICAN ENGINEER, RAN OUT OF GIN AND, FORCED TO IMPROVISE, CAME UP WITH THIS NOW-CLASSIC RUM-BASED CONCOCTION. GIVEN RUM'S STATUS AS THE HIGHLY ESTEEMED "MILK OF CUBA," IT'S LIKELY THIS COMBINATION HAD BEEN ENJOYED BEFORE THAT FATEFUL DAY, BUT IT TOOK AN AMERICAN TO LOUDLY ADVERTISE A GOOD THING.

SOON HAVANA BECAME THE DAIQUIRI CAPITAL OF THE WORLD, AND THE CITY'S EL FLORIDITA BAR WAS THE DRINK'S UNDISPUTED HEADQUARTERS. THERE, LEGENDARY BARTENDER CONSTANTE RIBAILAGUA INTRODUCED THE FROZEN VERSION AND ELEVATED THE DAIQUIRI TO PERFECTION. BY STRAIN-ING THE DRINK AFTER BLENDING IT WITH CRUSHED ICE, HE AVOIDED FURTHER DILUTION WHILE RETAINING THE FROSTY CHARACTER.

IN ITS PURE FORM, THE DAIQUIRI IS SIMPLE YET SUBLIME, BLENDING THE DELI-CATE SWEETNESS OF RUM WITH SUGAR AND THE JUICE OF ONE LIME. THE SECRET OF A PERFECT ONE IS NOT JUST IN THE BALANCE OF INGREDIENTS, BUT ALSO IN SQUEEZING THE LIME WITH YOUR FINGERS TO ALLOW THE OILS FROM THE PEEL TO MINGLE WITH THE JUICE, CREATING THE DAIQUIRI'S SIG-NATURE INTENSITY AND FLAVOR.

THE CLASSIC DAIQUIRI IS A GREAT BASE FOR IMPROVISATION AND CREATIVE MIXOLOGY. FROM LUSH GUAVA NECTAR TO SLICED BANANAS AND SPICED RUM, THIS SELECTION OF DAIQUIRI EMBELLISHMENTS PUSHES THE LIMITS.

THE COCOANUT GROOVE

Imagine that famous 1950s hot spot, the Cocoanut Grove, still open for business, complete with a DJ spinning island grooves for a suave clientele busy working up a thirst for a fabulous cocktail. The Cocoanut Groove would definitely qualify as the club's signature drink. Think of this as spiked coconut–Key lime pie in a glass. The coconut gelato is rich and creamy, while the sorbet makes for a lighter, frostier drink. When sweetness calls, this is the perfect after-dinner libation.

1½ **ounces Malibu rum**
½ **cup coconut sorbet or gelato**
1 **ounce fresh lime juice**
1 **ounce coconut milk (see page 13)**
1 **ounce pineapple juice**
½ **cup crushed ice**

GARNISH:
1 **pineapple wedge**
  Dusting of ground nutmeg

1. Chill a cocktail glass.

2. In a blender, combine the rum, sorbet, lime juice, coconut milk, pineapple juice, and ice. Blend until well combined and smooth.

3. Pour the mixture into the chilled glass. Place the pineapple wedge on the rim of the glass, dust the top of the drink with the nutmeg, and serve.

Serves 1

Quick Tip: For a great shortcut, substitute 2 ounces Knudsen's pineapple coconut beverage for the coconut milk and pineapple juice.

GUAVALUSCIOUS DAIQUIRI

This pink-hued flower of a drink has a subtle lime tang. The sweet perfumed flavor of guava nectar, with its tones of honey, melon, and strawberries, infused with the buttery warmth of Barbancourt rum results in a cocktail pleasantly reminiscent of pink grapefruits.

1¹/₂ cups cracked ice
  2 ounces Barbancourt rum or other gold rum
  3 ounces guava nectar
  ³/₄ ounce fresh lime juice
  1 tablespoon superfine sugar
  1 lime-peel spiral (see page 19) for garnish

1. Chill a large cocktail glass.

2. Fill a cocktail shaker with the ice and add the rum, guava nectar, lime juice, and sugar. Shake vigorously to blend and chill.

3. Strain the mixture into the chilled glass, place the lime-peel spiral on the rim of the glass, and serve.

Serves 1

PAPA HEMINGWAY'S DAIQUIRI

This legendary concoction fueled the imagination of Ernest Hemingway, the literary world's cocktail maven par excellence. Hemingway preferred his favorite Cuban cocktail without sugar, cold and sour, and with twice as much rum as the traditional daiquiri. This tangy variation of Papa's classic uses only 2 ounces of rum and permits the fresh-squeezed grapefruit juice flavor and sour cherry tones to shine through. But for those Papa-philes who must experience the original sin in its purest form, prepare this recipe with 3 ounces of silver rum. If you can find it, Havana Club Silver Dry is the way to go.

  ³/₄ ounce fresh lime juice
  1¹/₂ ounces fresh grapefruit juice
  ¹/₂ ounce maraschino liqueur
  2 ounces Cuban silver or other light rum
  1 cup crushed ice
  1 lime wedge for garnish

1. Chill a 6-ounce cocktail glass.

2. In a blender, combine the lime juice, grapefruit juice, maraschino liqueur, rum, and ice. Blend until well combined, frothy, and slightly slushy.

3. Pour the mixture into the chilled glass. Balance the lime wedge on the rim of the glass and serve.

Serves 1

52

GREEN FLASH

As all beachcombers know, on a cloudless evening, just as the sun goes down, a visually ephemeral moment called the green flash occurs. For two or three seconds, you can glimpse a green glow along the horizon. What better way to pass the time, waiting and watching (and watching and waiting) for that flash to appear, than enjoying this brilliant green drink. The herbal notes from Green Chartreuse impart a flavor reminiscent of a gin and tonic to this refreshing daiquiri.

1½ **cups cracked ice**

1½ **ounces silver rum**

¾ **ounce Green Chartreuse (herbal liqueur)**

¾ **ounce fresh lime juice**

1 **tablespoon superfine sugar**

6 **ice cubes**

2 to 3 **ounces club soda**

1 **tiny green orchid for garnish**

1. *Chill a tall 8-ounce glass.*

2. *Fill a cocktail shaker with the cracked ice and add the rum, Green Chartreuse, lime juice, and sugar. Shake vigorously to blend and chill.*

3. *Fill the chilled glass with the ice cubes and strain the mixture into the glass. Top off with the club soda.*

4. *Float the orchid on top and serve.*

Serves 1

BOSSA NOVA

Yes, you can actually power your Ford Fairlane with Brazilian cachaça, but I'd rather fuel a daiquiri with it, myself. This version mixes rum's fiery cousin (the one from Rio that tastes like trouble) with the brandy-orange warmth of Cointreau, a splash of tangy cranberry, and the mellow hazelnut flavor of Frangelico for a surprising chocolate-like finish. This frosty cocktail will get those dance-phobes gyrating.

1½ **ounces Cachaça 51**
1 **ounce Frangelico (hazelnut liqueur)**
½ **ounce Cointreau**
¾ **ounce fresh lime juice**
¾ **ounce cranberry juice**
1 **tablespoon honey**
1½ **cups crushed ice**
2 **cranberries for garnish**

1. *Chill a 6-ounce cocktail glass.*

2. *In a blender, combine the Cachaça, Frangelico, Cointreau, lime juice, cranberry juice, honey, and ice. Blend until well combined and slushy.*

3. *Pour into the chilled glass, float the cranberries in the drink, slip in a straw, and serve.*

Serves 1

COPABANANA DAIQUIRI

Island breeze meets urban savvy in this glamorous and velvety cocktail melding banana, raspberries, lime juice, and light rum. At once sweet, citrus spiked, and silky smooth, this sophisticated daiquiri captures the nostalgic magic of sipping tropical libations while listening to the sounds of Latin crooners beneath swaying palm fronds at the legendary 1940s Copacabana Nightclub.

4 **ounces Captain Morgan spiced rum**
1 **banana, peeled and sliced**
½ **cup fresh or frozen raspberries**
1 **ounce fresh lime juice**
2 **ounces sweet and sour (see page 28)**
1 **cup crushed ice**

GARNISH:
4 **fresh or frozen raspberries**
2 **lime wheels (see page 20)**

1. *Chill 2 large cocktail glasses.*

2. *In a blender, combine the rum, banana, raspberries, lime juice, and sweet and sour. Blend until well combined. Add the ice and blend until smooth.*

3. *Pour the mixture into the chilled glasses, dividing it evenly. Garnish each with 2 berries and a lime wheel and serve.*

Serves 2

ROYAL PALMS FLORI

CHAPTER 4

Classics

FROM CANCER
TO CAPRICORN

PIÑA COLADA NUEVA
DARK AND STORMY
SHAKE YOUR MOJITO
RAMOS GIN FIZZ
ZOMBIE
CLASSIC CAIPIRINHA
MAI TAI

LEGENDARY DRINKS OF THE TROPICS

THESE TROPICAL CLASSICS BLEW IN OFF THE BALMY TRADEWINDS. HAILING FROM EXOTIC LOCALES, THEY CAPTURE OUR ATTENTION WITH AMBROSIAL INGREDIENTS THAT QUENCH OUR THIRST FOR LIQUID ADVENTURE. FROM THE MYSTIQUE OF THE MINTY MOJITO TO THE MYTHOLOGICALLY POTENT ZOMBIE, THESE LEGENDARY DRINKS HAVE WITHSTOOD THE TEST OF TIME. CLASSIC COCKTAILS WITH PURE ISLAND ALCHEMY, THEY REFINE THE QUINTESSENTIAL FLAVORS OF THE EQUATORIAL LATITUDE. HERE, THEY ARE FORMULATED IN REVERENCE TO THE ORIGINALS, WITH A FEW TWEAKS TO ACHIEVE COSMOPOLITAN PERFECTION.

PIÑA COLADA NUEVA

Could the piña colada be any more luxurious and dreamy? Absolutely! This evolutionary version of the late 1950s Puerto Rican classic takes it from luxe to deluxe with the addition of passion-fruit liqueur and mango juice.

¹/₂ **cup diced pineapple**

2 **ounces silver rum**

1 **ounce Alizé de France (passion-fruit liqueur)**

1¹/₂ **ounces coconut cream (see page 13)**

1¹/₂ **ounces mango juice or nectar**

¹/₂ **ounce fresh lime juice**

1 **cup crushed ice**

GARNISH:

1 **pineapple slice**

1 **mango slice**

Shaved coconut (see page 13)

1. Chill a 10- to 12-ounce margarita glass or goblet.

2. In a blender, combine the pineapple, rum, Alizé de France, coconut cream, mango juice, lime juice, and ice. Blend until well combined and smooth.

3. Pour into the chilled glass. Using a cocktail pick, skewer the pineapple slice and mango slice together and balance on the rim of the glass. Top the drink with the shaved coconut and serve.

Serves 1

DARK AND STORMY ▶

This sparkling Bermuda favorite is known to combat the heat and soothe the stomach. Classically rich in the sweet, smoky molasses tones of Gosling's black rum and the tangy bite of Jamaican ginger beer (similar to ginger ale but with a stronger ginger flavor), it gets an extra kick of spice with the addition of fresh ginger.

4 **ice cubes**

1 or 2 **slices fresh ginger**

2 **ounces dark rum**

1 **ounce ginger syrup (see page 27)**

2 to 3 **ounces ginger beer**

¹/₂ **lime, cut into 2 wedges**

1. Chill an 8- to 10-ounce Old-Fashioned glass.

2. Fill the chilled glass with the ice and fresh ginger. Add the rum and ginger syrup and stir to combine.

3. Top off with the ginger beer. Squeeze the 2 lime wedges into the drink, drop them into the glass, and serve.

Serves 1

SHAKE YOUR MOJITO

Havana's delightfully refreshing answer to the mint julep has become a new classic in many American hot spots. Traditionally made by muddling mint in the glass, this drink, yet another Hemingway favorite, takes the "shaken not stirred" route to Havana heaven. My question: how many different cocktails can one man call his favorite?

Here are two different ways to prepare the mojito. One is the traditional method, and the other is a quick version. Both get you to the same place.

1 ounce fresh lime juice
1 tablespoon superfine sugar
6 to 8 fresh spearmint leaves
2 ounces white rum
6 ice cubes
3 to 4 ounces club soda, chilled

Traditional Version

1. *Chill an 8-ounce highball glass.*

2. *In the bottom of the chilled glass, combine the lime juice, sugar, and mint leaves, crushing them together with a bar spoon or muddler until the sugar is dissolved.*

3. *Add the rum, then fill the glass with the ice, top off with the club soda, and serve.*

Quick Version

1. *Chill an 8-ounce highball glass.*

2. *Fill a cocktail shaker with the ice and add the lime juice, sugar, mint leaves, and rum. Shake vigorously to blend and chill.*

3. *Take the top off the shaker and pour the mixture, ice and all, into the chilled glass. Top off with the club soda and serve.*

Serves 1

Variations: For an equally refreshing mint-based drink, try the mojito with gin instead of rum. Also look for lemon or orange mint—experimint!

RAMOS GIN FIZZ

The Ramos brothers ushered this classy cocktail into popularity in the 1890s, where it became the signature libation at the Imperial Cabinet Saloon in New Orleans. This sultry Gulf Coast variation calls for the Ramos brothers' secret ingredient: orange flower water. You can be glamorously vintage and shake this in a cocktail shaker for four or five minutes, or expediently modern and whirl it in a blender (omitting the ice). Either way, your time-honored cocktail won't disappoint. So pop Bogey's *Dead Reckoning* into the VCR, sit back, and take a trip to New Orleans, that hex-filled capital of jazz and jambalaya.

1½ **cups cracked ice or 6 ice cubes**
1½ **ounces gin**
1 **ounce fresh lemon juice**
½ **ounce fresh lime juice**
2 **teaspoons vanilla extract**
3 or 4 **dashes orange flower water**
1 **egg white (optional)**
1½ **ounces heavy cream or half-and-half**
1 **tablespoon superfine sugar**
2 to 4 **ounces club soda, chilled**

GARNISH:
1 **lemon slice**
1 **small pink orchid**

1. *Chill a highball glass.*

2. *Fill a cocktail shaker with the ice and add the gin, lemon juice, lime juice, vanilla, orange flower water, egg white (if using), cream, and sugar. Shake vigorously until well blended and frothy, 4 or 5 minutes.*

3. *Strain the mixture into the chilled glass, and top off with the club soda. Using a cocktail pick, skewer the lemon slice and orchid together and balance on the rim of the glass, then serve.*

Serves 1

ZOMBIE

Don the Beachcomber's mind-altering concoction, which has been subject to variation since its conception in 1934, always posed a challenge for creative mixologists to reach their idea of the perfect Zombie. Not surprisingly, given the euphoric reaction of a country just coming out of Prohibition, the Beachcomber's Zombie went all out, combining three types of rum—light, gold, and dark—with a blend of fresh fruit juices. I found that this particular recipe turns out a deceivingly smooth and fruity glass of velvet dynamite, one easily fitting Don's house rule of "only two per customer."

1½ **cups cracked ice or 6 ice cubes**
  1 **ounce Puerto Rican light rum**
  1 **ounce gold rum**
  1 **ounce Jamaican dark rum**
  1 **ounce passion fruit syrup**
  1 **ounce crème de banana**
  1 **ounce pineapple juice**
  1 **ounce fresh lemon juice**
  1 **ounce fresh lime juice**
  1 **tablespoon brown sugar**
½ **ounce grenadine**
½ **ounce 151-proof Demerara rum**

GARNISH:
  1 **pineapple wedge**
  1 **lime wheel (see page 20)**
  1 **green orchid**
  1 **cherry**

1. Chill a 16-ounce hurricane or Zombie glass.

2. Fill a cocktail shaker with the ice and add all the ingredients except the 151-proof rum and the garnishes. Shake vigorously to blend and chill.

3. Take the top off the shaker and pour the mixture, ice and all, into the chilled glass. Float the 151-proof rum on top of the drink.

4. Using a cocktail pick, skewer the pineapple, lime, green orchid, and cherry together and balance on the rim of the glass, then serve.

Serves 1

CLASSIC CAIPIRINHA

The name of this Brazilian classic, loosely translated as "country bumpkin" or "little peasant girl," refers to its "uncivilized" preparation in the same glass from which it will be sipped. As you muddle the limes against the sugar in the bottom of the heavy glass, the fragrant oils from the crushed citrus peels are released. Cachaça, the fiery Brazilian spirit distilled directly from raw sugarcane, gives the drink its distinctive bite. Put on Brazil 66 and muddle to the beat of the bossa nova.

4 or 5 lime wedges

2 teaspoons granulated sugar or turbinado sugar

1 cup cracked ice

2 ounces cachaça

1. *Place the lime wedges in a thick-bottomed Old-Fashioned glass and sprinkle the sugar over them.*

2. *Using the back of a bar spoon or a muddler, crush the sugar and limes together until the sugar is dissolved and the lime juice is released.*

3. *Add the ice and pour in the cachaça. Stir a few revolutions and serve.*

Serves 1

MAI TAI

One of the dangers in dealing with many of the true classics in the tropical drink genre is that clichés abound. But when that classic lives up to its archetypal roots, you simply have to say so. The original Trader Vic's mai tai recipe from 1944, so much simpler than the current "Hawaiian punch" transmutations, deserves its Tahitian title, which means "out of this world." Martinique rhum vieux is the ideal component in this drink but hard to find in the United States, so if you cannot get hold of a bottle, any fine aged rum will work just as well.

1½ **cups cracked ice**
1½ **ounces Myers's dark or other dark Jamaican rum**
  1 **ounce Martinique rhum vieux or other aged rum**
 ½ **ounce orange curaçao**
 ¼ **ounce simple syrup (see page 27)**
 ½ **ounce orgeat or other almond-flavored syrup**
 ½ **ounce fresh orange juice**
1¼ **ounces fresh lime juice**
  6 **ice cubes**

GARNISH:
  1 **orange-peel spiral (see page 19)**
  1 **small purple orchid**

1. *Chill a 10- to 12-ounce Collins glass.*

2. *Fill a cocktail shaker with the cracked ice and add the rums, curaçao, simple syrup, orgeat, orange juice, and lime juice. Shake vigorously to blend and chill.*

3. *Fill the chilled glass with the ice cubes and strain the mixture over the ice. Float the orange-peel spiral and orchid in the drink and serve.*

Serves 1

CHAPTER 5

Exotica

CONSIDER THESE COCKTAILS A LIQUID EXPLORATION INTO UNCHARTED TERRITORIES—LANDS TEEMING WITH INTRIGUING AND ECCENTRIC FRUITS AND SPICES INDIGENOUS TO THE TROPICS. EACH INGREDIENT, FROM THE FRAGRANT CARIBBEAN TAMARIND NECTAR USED IN THE SHARK BITE TO THE CITRUSY TANG OF THE PAN-ASIAN KUMQUAT IN THE SHANGHAI SLING, DELIVERS ITS OWN DELICIOUSLY DISTINCT FLAVOR. WHEN FORAGING FOR THESE EXOTIC INGREDIENTS, LOOK IN SPECIALTY GOURMET, ASIAN, OR LATIN MARKETS. WEB SITES LIKE WWW.ASIAFOODS.COM ALSO OFFER MANY EXOTIC FRUITS, NECTARS, HERBS, AND SPICES.

SHARK BITE

PEARL FROM IPANEMA

METAXA MANGO SIDECAR

TOBAGO COCONUT FLIP

SHANGHAI SLING

BALI HIGHBALL

SHARK BITE

This surprising sweep of flavors comes together swimmingly in a sassy citrus cocktail that will have you circling around for a second. Sharp silver tequila is fused with the rich flavors of molasses and anise from mauby (a favorite Caribbean beverage made from the bark of small trees), the fragrant, lemon-tea-like essence of tamarind, and the sweet and mellow bouquet of crimson-hued blood orange juice. You can find canned tamarind nectar and mauby drink concentrate (to be diluted to taste) at most Latin markets. Blood oranges have become increasingly available in the produce sections of many supermarkets.

1½ **cups cracked ice or 6 ice cubes**

1½ **ounces good-quality silver tequila**

1½ **ounces fresh blood orange juice**

1 **ounce fresh lemon juice**

1 **ounce tamarind nectar**

¾ **ounce Grand Marnier**

½ **teaspoon mauby drink concentrate**

1 **lemon-peel spiral
(see page 19) for garnish**

1. Chill a large cocktail glass.

2. Fill a cocktail shaker with the ice and add the tequila, blood orange juice, lemon juice, tamarind nectar, Grand Marnier, and mauby concentrate. Shake vigorously to blend and chill.

3. Strain the mixture into the chilled glass. Drop in the lemon-peel spiral and serve.

Serves 1

PEARL FROM IPANEMA

Rio may be red hot, but this is one cool cocktail. A melding of Brazilian flavors float together in this shimmering pink dream, to create a drink as stylish as the beauty on the beach and as lively as carnival. You will want to use true grenadine, which is made from pomegranates, not that ersatz bottled stuff that's colored red and sweetened with corn syrup.

Superfine sugar rim (see page 22)

1½ **cups cracked ice or 6 ice cubes**

1½ **ounces cachaça**

2 **ounces guanabana juice**

1 **ounce KéKé Beach (lime liqueur)**

½ **ounce fresh lemon juice**

1 **teaspoon pomegranate syrup
(grenadine)**

1 **lime-peel twist (see page 20)
for garnish**

1. Coat the rim of a large chilled cocktail glass with sugar. Chill until needed.

2. Fill a cocktail shaker with the ice and add the cachaça, guanabana juice, lime liqueur, lemon juice, and pomegranate syrup. Shake vigorously to blend and chill.

3. Strain the mixture into the prepared glass. Twist the lime peel over the drink, drop it in, and serve.

Serves 1

Note: If you have trouble finding the KéKé Beach, substitute 1 ounce fresh lime juice.

METAXA MANGO SIDECAR

The Sidecar takes an exotic excursion to the Greek Islands. This smooth-sailing variation on the classic melds the velvety Cognac tones of metaxa, the fragrance of mango, and the zing of lemon and lime into a drink so transporting, you may never return to the basic Sidecar again. This innovative cocktail is a specialty at OBA!, a tropical oasis in Portland, Oregon.

> **Superfine sugar rim (see page 22)**
> 1 **cup cubed mango**
> 3 **ounces metaxa**
> 3 **ounces sweet and sour (see page 28)**
> 2 **ounces mango juice**
> 1 **ounce fresh orange juice**
> 1 **cup crushed ice**
> 2 **lemon wheels (see page 20) for garnish**

1. Coat the rims of 2 large chilled cocktail glasses with sugar. Chill until needed.

2. In a blender, combine the cubed mango, metaxa, sweet and sour, mango juice, orange juice, and ice. Blend until smooth.

3. Pour the mixture into the prepared glasses, dividing it evenly. Place a lemon wheel on the rim of each glass and serve.

Serves 2

TOBAGO COCONUT FLIP

This flavor combo will flip your canoe. Frothy and creamy, with an intriguing blend of rich coconut and zippy cinnamon, it tastes like a Christmas holiday on a remote island in the Pacific. If you are a cinnamon fanatic, try this recipe with an additional 1/4 ounce Goldschläger, the Swiss cinnamon liqueur that reveals a swirl of gold-leaf bits when stirred. It's a trip to spicy bliss.

> **Coconut-shell cup (see page 20) (optional)**
> 1 1/2 **cups cracked ice or 6 ice cubes**
> 1 1/2 **ounces Malibu rum**
> 1 **ounce coconut milk (see page 13)**
> 1/4 **ounce Goldschläger (cinnamon liqueur)**

GARNISH:
> **Dusting of ground cinnamon**
> 1 **orange blossom**

1. Chill a coconut-shell cup or large cocktail glass.

2. Fill a cocktail shaker with the ice and add the Malibu rum, coconut milk, and Goldschläger. Shake vigorously to blend and chill.

3. Strain the mixture into the chilled coconut-shell cup or glass. Top with a dusting of cinnamon, float the orange blossom on the surface, slip in a straw, and serve.

Serves 1

SHANGHAI SLING

Although this enticing little number may not loosen your resistance to life on the high seas, the pure alchemy of citrus, gin's juniper tones, and the sweet black raspberry of Chambord will surely shanghai your senses. The Asian influence of frozen kumquats lends a visually elegant element and an extra citrus kick.

1½ **cups cracked ice**

2 **ounces good-quality gin**

¾ **ounce kumquat syrup (see page 27)**

1 **ounce sweet and sour (see page 28)**

6 **ice cubes**

2 **frozen poached kumquats (see page 27)**

Splash of Chambord (black raspberry liqueur)

3 to 4 **ounces club soda, chilled**

GARNISH:

1 **lime slice**

1 **kumquat flower (see page 21)**

1. *Chill a 10- to 12-ounce glass.*

2. *Fill a cocktail shaker with the cracked ice and add the gin, kumquat syrup, and sweet and sour. Shake vigorously to blend and chill.*

3. *Fill the chilled glass with the ice cubes and add the frozen kumquats. Strain the mixture into the glass.*

4. *Add the Chambord and top off with the club soda. Using a cocktail pick, skewer the lime slice and kumquat flower together, balance on the rim of the glass, and serve with a straw.*

Serves 1

BALI HIGHBALL

It's time you to let your thoughts float away into some distant moonlit cove, and there's no better vehicle for doing that than this effervescent ambrosia. The fragrantly sweet juices of lychee and hibiscus are paired with gin and a touch of lime juice for the zing factor. One sip of this highball and you are transported straight to a blue lagoon and into a canoe with Bing Crosby crooning "Bali Hai." Technically, the typical highball involves only two ingredients, but true to the tropical cocktail tradition, we are gilding the lily here.

1½ cups cracked ice
3 ounces gin
4 ounces lychee juice
1 ounce fresh lime juice
1 ounce hibiscus syrup (see page 27)
12 ice cubes
4 to 6 ounces club soda, chilled

GARNISH:
2 lime slices
2 pink hibiscuses

1 Chill 2 highball glasses.

2. Fill a cocktail shaker with the cracked ice and add the gin, lychee juice, lime juice, and hibiscus syrup. Shake vigorously to blend and chill.

3. Fill the chilled glasses with 6 ice cubes each. Strain the mixture into the glasses, dividing it evenly. Top off with the club soda.

4. Using a cocktail pick, skewer a lime slice and a flower together and balance on the rim of each glass, then serve.

Serves 2

CHAPTER 6

Mambo
MARGARITAS

BITE OF THE IGUANA
MADAGASCAR MOOD SHIFTER
PAPAYARITA
BONSAI MARGARITA
PRICKLY AGAVE

DRINKS WITH LIQUID RHYTHM

MANY TALES SURROUND THE CONCEPTION OF THE MARGARITA. SUFFICE IT TO SAY, EVERYONE WHO EVER KNEW A WOMAN NAMED MARGARITA AND OWNED A SHAKER HAS CLAIMED TO BE THE ORIGINATOR. AS THE 1930S AND 1940S HEATED UP WITH AN INFATUATION FOR ANYTHING LATIN, BARTENDERS SHAKING TO THE MAMBO BEAT PROPELLED FIERY TEQUILA INTO THE NOW-CLASSIC MARGARITA COCKTAIL.

THE KEY TO THE ULTIMATE MARGARITA IS FRESH-SQUEEZED LIME JUICE COMBINED WITH 100 PERCENT AGAVE TEQUILA AND A PREMIUM ORANGE LIQUEUR. OPPOSING LOYALIST CAMPS DEBATE SERVING IT ON THE ROCKS VERSUS FROZEN, AND PURISTS INSIST ON A SALT RIM.

A MARGARITA MADE WITH ROSE'S LIME JUICE OR A PREBOTTLED MARGARITA MIX WOULD BE BOOTED OUT OF EITHER CAMP. AN ACCEPTABLE ALTERNATIVE TO FRESH-SQUEEZED LIME JUICE IS FROZEN LIMEADE, WHICH MAKES A GREAT SHORTCUT WITH SWEETNESS AS AN ADDED BONUS. WITH ITS SIMPLE LIME AND TEQUILA BASE, THE MARGARITA IS AN IDEAL VEHICLE FOR EXPLORING NEW EXOTIC CONCOCTIONS.

BITE OF THE IGUANA

Whoo-ee! For those with an unwavering affection for spicy Bloody Marys and tangy margaritas, look no further. Made with hot-and-spicy pepper-infused tequila, sweet orange cherry tomatoes from Mexico, and fresh seasonings, this zippy cocktail will give you the feeling something just bit you, and you liked it!

Salt rim (see page 22)
1½ **ounces pepper tequila (see page 30)**
¾ **ounce Triple Sec or other orange liqueur**
1½ **ounces sweet and sour (see page 28)**
½ **cup stemmed and halved orange cherry tomatoes**
1 **clove garlic, finely minced**
1 **green onion, chopped**
2 or 3 **dashes Worcestershire sauce**
¾ **cup crushed ice**

GARNISH:
1 **lime wedge**
2 **orange cherry tomatoes**

1. Coat the rim of a chilled 6-ounce margarita glass with salt. Chill until needed.

2. In a blender, combine the tequila, Triple Sec, sweet and sour, halved tomatoes, garlic, green onion, Worcestershire sauce, and ice. Blend until smooth.

3. Pour the mixture into the prepared glass. Using a cocktail pick, skewer a lime wedge between the 2 tomatoes and balance on the rim of the glass, then serve.

Serves 1

MADAGASCAR MOOD SHIFTER

As a hot wind blows through Madagascar, the locals know the secret to beating the heat: a frisky blend of cooling mint teamed with chilled tangerine juice, aromatic orange flavor from Citrónge liqueur, and vanilla bean–infused tequila. Sipping this serene cocktail will lower the mercury-induced madness.

1 1/2 **cups cracked ice or 6 ice cubes**
1 1/2 **ounces vanilla tequila (see page 30)**
3/4 **ounce Citrónge (orange liqueur)**
2 **ounces fresh tangerine juice**
1 **ounce sweet and sour (see page 28)**
3 or 4 **fresh mint leaves**

GARNISH:
1 **tangerine slice**
1 **fresh mint sprig**

1. Chill a large cocktail glass.

2. Fill a cocktail shaker with the ice and add the tequila, Citrónge, tangerine juice, sweet and sour, and mint leaves. Shake vigorously to blend and chill.

3. Strain the mixture into the chilled glass. Using a cocktail pick, skewer the tangerine slice and the mint sprig together and balance on the rim of the glass, then serve.

Serves 1

PAPAYARITA

You've traveled to some remote crescent of beach to escape the urban frenzy. But there is no rest for the weary. Damp, sandy, sun-worshiping compadres are hogging your beach blanket. Distract them with this refreshing pitcher of papaya-rich margaritas. Replacing the usual Triple Sec with Damiana liqueur, a legendary herbal aphrodisiac, will ensure your spot in the sun.

2 **cups cubed papaya**
6 **ounces sweet and sour (see page 28)**
6 **ounces good-quality silver tequila**
2 **ounces Damiana (herbal liqueur)**
1 1/2 **cups crushed ice**

GARNISH:
6 **lime wedges**
6 **small pink orchids**

1. Chill 6 margarita glasses.

2. In a blender, combine the papaya, sweet and sour, tequila, and Damiana. Blend until thoroughly pureed. Add the ice and blend until the mixture is smooth.

3. Pour the mixture into the chilled glasses, dividing it evenly. Using a cocktail pick, skewer a lime wedge and an orchid together and balance on the rim of each glass, then serve.

Serves 6

78

BONSAI MARGARITA

A fusion of Oriental and Occidental flavors are at play in this Pacific Rim cocktail, adding a cosmopolitan entry into the margarita domain. The aggressive mingling of sweet and fruity with tangy and sour will enchant those who love the muskmelon flavor of Midori.

Salt rim (see page 22)
1½ **cups cracked ice**
3 **ounces Midori (melon liqueur)**
1 **ounce silver tequila**
1 **ounce Harlequin (orange liqueur)**
3 **ounces fresh lime juice**
2 **tablespoons superfine sugar**
10 to 12 **ice cubes**
2 **lemon-peel twists**
(see page 20) for garnish

1. Coat the rims of 2 chilled margarita glasses with salt. Chill until needed.

2. Fill a cocktail shaker with the cracked ice and add the Midori, tequila, Harlequin, lime juice, and sugar. Shake vigorously to blend and chill.

3. Fill the prepared glasses with the ice cubes. Strain the mixture into the glasses, dividing it evenly. Twist a lemon peel over each drink, drop it in, and serve.

Serves 2

PRICKLY AGAVE

This highly sophisticated desert libation mixes the prickly sharpness of silver agave juice, the sweet-tart juices of prickly-pear juice, and the orange, almond, and vanilla tones from Tuaca liqueur to produce a margarita with pure liquid rhythm. Look for prickly-pear juice in specialty and natural foods markets.

Sugar and salt rim (see page 22)
1½ cups cracked ice or 6 ice cubes
1½ ounces good-quality silver tequila
1 ounce Tuaca (citrus liqueur)
2 ounces prickly-pear juice
1 ounce fresh lime juice
1 lime-peel spiral
(see page 19) for garnish

1. Coat the rim of a chilled margarita or large cocktail glass with salt and sugar. Chill until needed.

2. Fill a cocktail shaker with the ice and add the tequila, Tuaca, prickly-pear juice, and lime juice. Shake vigorously to blend and chill.

3. Strain the mixture into the prepared glass. Drop in the lime spiral and serve.

Serves 1

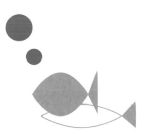

CHAPTER 7

Mixing
UNDER THE STARS

FROM THE MOMENT LOUIS-ANTOINE DE BOUGAINVILLE, THE FRENCH EXPEDITION LEADER, CAUGHT HIS FIRST GLIMPSE OF UNINHIBITED TAHITIANS IN 1767 AND REPORTED BACK WITH TALES OF FREE-LOVING ISLANDERS, THE NATURAL CONCLUSION WAS DRAWN: THE LUSH, HIBISCUS-STREWN PARADISE OF A DISTANT PINK SHORE HELD THE PROMISE OF PASSIONS PURSUED WITH RECKLESS ABANDON. AND THIS WAS LONG BEFORE CLUB MED! LET THESE STEAMY TONICS FROM THE SULTRY ZONE STOKE THE FIRES AND, WHO KNOWS, THEY MIGHT JUST FUEL YOUR DESIRE TO EMBRACE YOUR NATURAL URGES.

FIG LEAF FIZZ

VELVET VOODOO

BETWEEN THE SHEETS

BANANA-COGNAC BLISS

RIKI TIKI TODDY

MARTINIQUE MUSE

FIG LEAF FIZZ

Let's get down to the primordial basics, here thinly veiled in a sparkling glass of urban sophistication. Not intended for the modest recluse, this cocktail is as extroverted as they come. Made with premium vodka such as Grey Goose for the perfection factor, the heady combination of chocolate, vanilla, and orange is known to loosen inhibitions—and fig leaves.

1½ **cups cracked ice**

1½ **ounces good-quality vodka**

½ **ounce Tuaca (vanilla-citrus liqueur)**

½ **ounce crème de cacao**

6 **ice cubes**

2 to 3 **ounces sparkling tangerine or orange beverage**

GARNISH:

1 **orange wheel (see page 20)**

1 **fresh mint sprig**

1. *Fill a cocktail shaker with the cracked ice and add the vodka, Tuaca, and crème de cacao. Shake vigorously to blend and chill.*

2. *Fill a tall 10-ounce glass with the ice cubes and strain the mixture into the glass. Top off with the sparkling tangerine beverage and stir a few revolutions.*

3. *Garnish the rim of the glass with the orange wheel and mint and serve.*

Serves 1

VELVET VOODOO

This taste of pure island magic will lull you into a languid state of mind. Buttery-rich Haitian rum stoked with the infamous absinthe (refined and available again) combine to make the perfect nightcap—a powerful potion that conjures up Screamin' Jay Hawkins crooning "I Put a Spell on You."

> **3 ounces Barbancourt rum**
> **1 ounce absinthe or Pernod (anise liqueur)**
> **1 ounce amaretto**
> **1/2 cup vanilla ice cream, softened**
> **1 cup crushed ice**

GARNISH:

> **Dusting of ground nutmeg**
> **Semisweet chocolate**

1. In a blender, combine the rum, absinthe, amaretto, and ice cream. Blend until well combined and creamy. Add the ice and blend until smooth.

2. Pour the mixture into 2 glasses, dividing it evenly. Dust each drink with the nutmeg and shave some chocolate over the top, then serve.

Serves 2

BETWEEN THE SHEETS

Think Egyptian cotton adorned with palm trees, and imagine the gentle roar of the surf on a moonlit night, a balmy breeze, and this smooth-as-silk aphrodisiac. Warm spicy tones, a pleasant hint of zesty lemon, and the heady island flavor of Demerara rum from Guyana come together in this seductive concoction. Who knows, it might just lead you . . . hence, the name.

> **Superfine sugar rim (see page 22)**
> **1 1/2 cups cracked ice or 6 ice cubes**
> **1 1/2 ounces brandy**
> **1 1/2 ounces Grand Marnier**
> **1 ounce Demerara or other dark rum**
> **1 ounce fresh lemon juice**
> **2 lemon-peel twists (see page 20) for garnish**

1. Coat the rims of two 6-ounce chilled cocktail glasses with sugar. Chill until needed.

2. Fill a cocktail shaker with the ice and add the brandy, Grand Marnier, rum, and lemon juice. Shake vigorously to blend and chill.

3. Strain the mixture into the prepared glasses, dividing it evenly. Twish the lemon peel over the drink, drop it in, and serve.

Serves 2

BANANA-COGNAC BLISS

Creamy and aromatic, this tropical cordial is the answer to that after-dinner craving for something delectable but not too heavy, something light but just rich enough to satisfy. This lovely cocktail blends the warmth of Cognac and banana liqueur with the sweetness of ice cream, and adds a splash of club soda for a bubbly dessert-in-a-glass. Served on a moonlit, sultry night, the chocolate accent will melt any defenses.

2 ounces Cognac
1¹/₂ ounces crème de banana
1 cup vanilla ice cream, softened
3 ounces club soda, chilled
Semisweet chocolate for garnish

1. In a blender, combine the Cognac, crème de banana, and ice cream. Blend until smooth. Add the club soda and blend for just a few seconds.

2. Pour the mixture into 2 large cocktail glasses, dividing it evenly. Shave some chocolate over the top of each drink and serve.

Serves 2

RIKI TIKI TODDY

This mischievous drink will have you slinking around in the balmy night. Warmed with spiced rum and sweet Drambuie laced with hints of honey and heather, you will be spirited away by a toddy that tastes playful and naughty.

¹/₂ cup water
1¹/₂ ounces spiced rum
¹/₂ ounce Drambuie
¹/₂ ounce Grand Marnier
1 tablespoon honey
1¹/₂ ounces coconut milk (see page 13)
Pinch of ground cloves

GARNISH:
Dollop of whipped cream
1 lemon wedge studded with whole cloves

1. In a small saucepan, bring the water to a boil.

2. In a heatproof mug, combine the rum, Drambuie, Grand Marnier, honey, coconut milk, and ground cloves. Stir until well blended.

3. Add the boiling water and stir until the honey is dissolved.

4. Top with the whipped cream. Garnish the rim with the clove-studded lemon wedge and serve.

Serves 1

MARTINIQUE MUSE

French influence is pervasive on the island of Martinique, and Parfait Amour, the lavender-scented liqueur with flavors of violet and orange (reportedly once served in the more refined French brothels), is always in synch with the languorous island life. A sultry love potion if ever there was one, this heady mixture is known for its libido-stimulating properties. In short, this is ideal for sipping beneath a canopy of stars.

1½ cups cracked ice or 6 ice cubes
1 ounce Stolichnaya orange vodka
1 ounce Parfait Amour (violet-citrus liqueur)
2 to 3 ounces Champagne, chilled
2 to 4 orange blossom petals or violet flowers for garnish

1. Chill 2 Champagne flutes.

2. Fill a cocktail shaker with the ice and add the vodka and Parfait Amour. Shake vigorously to blend and chill.

3. Strain the mixture into the chilled flutes, dividing it evenly. Slowly top off each glass with the Champagne.

4. Float the orange blossom petals or violets in each drink and serve.

Serves 2

88

CHAPTER 8

Virgin Island

HIBISCUS-LEMONGRASS ICED TEA COOLER

MANGO TANGO

JAMAICAN BANANA-MOCHA SHAKE

SAMOAN SMOOTHIE

COCONUT FLOAT

KIWI-PINEAPPLE KISS

SUMPTUOUS SMOOTHIES WITHOUT THE SPIRITS

YOU CAN TAKE THE JUNGLE OUT OF THE JUICE AND STILL HAVE FUN IN THE SUN QUAFFING THESE ALCOHOL-FREE ELIXIRS THAT WILL KEEP YOU UPRIGHT AND SURFING QUASIMODO-STYLE FOR HOURS. THIS THIRST-QUENCHING SELECTION OF ENERGIZING FRAPPÉS AND TROPICAL CLASSICS IS TAILOR-MADE FOR THOSE WHO WOULD RATHER CATCH THAT EUPHORIC RUSH BY BRAVING A MONSTER WAVE.

HIBISCUS-LEMONGRASS ICED TEA COOLER

Lemongrass has long been a popular Thai ingredient, bringing the sweet, fragrant, delicate aroma of lemon to many recipes. It is also known as a soothing digestive when steeped. Sipping this spicy iced tea, which combines the sweetness of lemongrass syrup with the tartness of vibrant red hibiscus, is a lovely way to cool down. Indeed, you may just breeze the whole afternoon away.

- **4 cups water**
- **6 tablespoons loose hibiscus tea, or 6 hibiscus tea bags**
- **1 cinnamon stick, broken into pieces**
- **Grated zest of 1 orange**
- **1/2 cup lemongrass syrup (see page 27)**
- **2 trays ice cubes (28 to 32)**
- **4 lemongrass stalks for garnish**

1. In a saucepan or teakettle, bring the water to boil.

2. Place the tea, cinnamon, orange zest, and lemongrass syrup in a teapot, and then pour in the boiling water. Let stand until cool.

3. Fill 4 tall glasses with the ice. Strain the tea over the ice, dividing it evenly among the glasses. Garnish each glass with a lemongrass stalk for stirring.

Serves 4

Tip: Lemongrass syrup is great to have on hand in summer for making a light thirst quencher. Just add a few tablespoons to a glass of ice and top off with club soda.

MANGO TANGO

Here's a formula that's sure to plunge the entire crowd into the tropical fundamentals. Whatever you do, don't skip the ginger syrup, as it transforms this already great Sunday-morning fruit drink into the Friday-night fun punch it is meant to be. Some have been known to cheat and slip in a little banana liqueur, but let's keep this baby sacrosanct, shall we? You can find premade ginger syrup in some supermarkets, but the fresh-made is best.

- **2 ounces fresh lime juice**
- **1 ounce ginger syrup (see page 27)**
- **1 cup cubed mango**
- **1 cup cubed pineapple**
- **2 cups cracked ice or 10 to 12 ice cubes**
- **4 to 6 ounces club soda, chilled**

GARNISH:
- **2 mango slices**
- **2 pineapple wedges**

1. Chill 2 tall 10-ounce glasses.

2. In a blender, combine the lime juice, ginger syrup, mango, and pineapple. Blend until well combined and smooth.

3. Fill the chilled glasses with the ice. Pour the mixture into the glasses, dividing it evenly. Top off each glass with club soda.

4. Using a cocktail pick, skewer a mango slice and a pineapple wedge together and balance on the rim of each glass, then serve.

Serves 2

JAMAICAN BANANA-MOCHA SHAKE

It doesn't get any better than this. Java, chocolate, and island spices are blended with the zesty citrus of Jamaican ugli-fruit juice to produce a drink rich in flavor, yet frothy and light from the addition of club soda. This is the ultimate pre–reggae party blend-it-up-baby chocolate–fruit punch. Yah mon!

1 **banana, peeled and sliced**

½ **cup coffee ice cream, softened**

3 **ounces fresh ugli-fruit juice or orange juice**

2 **tablespoons chocolate syrup**

1 **tablespoon vanilla extract**

   Pinch of ground cinnamon

   Pinch of ground cardamom

4 **ounces club soda**

1 **cup crushed ice**

GARNISH:

2 **citrus slices**

2 **banana slices**

1. *Chill 2 tall 10-ounce glasses.*

2. *In a blender, combine the banana, ice cream, ugli-fruit juice, chocolate syrup, vanilla, cinnamon, cardamom, club soda, and ice. Blend until well combined and smooth.*

3. *Pour the mixture into the chilled glasses, dividing it evenly. Using a cocktail pick, skewer a citrus slice and a banana slice together and balance on the rim of each glass, then serve with straws.*

Serves 2

Variation: For a malted version, add 2 tablespoons malt powder.

SAMOAN SMOOTHIE

This smoothie will help you cool down after an intense day of fire dancing or coconut harvesting. As papayas go, the Strawberry papaya is queen. Surpassing the regular variety with a superior sweetness and lush, creamy texture, it adds an ambrosial touch to this Polynesian refreshment.

- **1 banana, peeled and sliced**
- **1 cup cubed Strawberry papaya**
- **1 cup (8 ounces) passion-fruit juice, chilled**
- **1½ ounces fresh lemon juice**
- **½ cup crushed ice**

GARNISH:
- **2 Strawberry papaya slices**
- **2 banana slices**

1. Chill 2 tall 10-ounce glasses.

2. In a blender, combine the sliced banana, cubed papaya, passion-fruit juice, lemon juice, and ice. Blend until smooth.

3. Pour the mixture into the chilled glasses, dividing it evenly. Using a cocktail pick, skewer a papaya slice and a banana slice together and balance on the rim of each glass, then serve.

Serves 2

COCONUT FLOAT

Coconuts do float, and this frosty after-dinner treat will float you straight to a palm-peppered paradise. Perfect on a hot summer day, or for when the occasion calls for a dessert that is bubbly and light, this creamy concoction is the ticket to island decadence.

- **3/4 cup coconut sorbet or gelato, softened**
- **Splash of raspberry syrup**
- **3 to 4 ounces Jamaican ginger beer or ginger ale, chilled**
- **A few raspberries for garnish**

1. Drop the coconut sorbet into a tall glass, add the raspberry syrup, and top off with the ginger beer.

2. Float a few raspberries in the drink and serve with a straw.

Serves 1

KIWI-PINEAPPLE KISS

You say *liquado*, I say *batido*. These creamy refreshers from the Latin sun belt are a lighter, smoothie-like answer to the milk shake. Using fresh fruit as its main ingredient, the Spanish *batido* calls for ice and a splash of cream or sweetened condensed milk, while the Mexican *liquado* is made with milk and honey. This particular recipe is the best of both worlds. Pick your fruit: the pineapple in combination with the mint is marvelous, but also try this recipe with any of your favorite blendable fruit, such as mangoes, peaches, strawberries, or blueberries.

1	**kiwifruit, peeled and diced**
1½	**cups diced pineapple**
½	**ounce fresh lime juice**
2	**tablespoons coconut cream (see page 13)**
2	**tablespoons honey**
2	**tablespoons half-and-half**
4 to 6	**fresh mint leaves**
1½	**cups crushed ice**

GARNISH:

1	**pineapple wedge**
1	**lime slice**

1. *Chill a tall 10- to 12-ounce glass.*

2. *In a blender, combine the kiwifruit, pineapple, lime juice, coconut cream, honey, half-and-half, mint leaves, and ice. Blend until smooth.*

3. *Pour the mixture into the chilled glass. Using a cocktail pick, skewer the pineapple wedge and lime slice together and balance on the rim of the glass, then serve.*

Serves 1

CHAPTER 9

Havana

GOOD TIME

CUBISIMO COCKTAIL PARTY

BALINESE SOIRÉE

POLYNESIAN SPA PARTY

URBAN LUAU MADNESS

TROPICAL TANGO FOR TWO

SOIRÉES FOR THE SOPHISTICATED SAVAGE

FOR THOSE WHO LONG FOR THE BALMY BREEZES OF THE PACIFIC, AND WANT TO GIVE THOSE POTTED PALMS IN THE CORNER OF THE LIVING ROOM A REASON TO LIVE, A STEAMY TROPICAL FETE CAN BE JUST THE ANSWER. FROM A SOPHISTICATED AND SWANK BALINESE SOIRÉE TO A MOCK-SERIOUS CUBAN EXPATRIATE AFFAIR, THIS SECTION WILL INSPIRE YOUR DESIRE TO SHAKE FROSTY COCKTAILS IN AN ISLAND SCENE.

SETTING THE TROPICAL STAGE WITH A FEW KEY PROPS, FROM LUSH FLORA AND EXOTIC ARTIFACTS TO ACTUALLY DRAGGING THE CANOE INTO THE LIVING ROOM, WILL HELP CONJURE UP THAT ISLAND EXPERIENCE. THE AMBIENCE CAN BE FABULOUSLY ELABORATE OR AS SIMPLE AS TURNING ON A CEILING FAN AND DIMMING THE LIGHTS. THIS SECTION OFFERS UP CREATIVE SUGGESTIONS FOR DÉCOR, INVENTIVE INVITATIONS, THE PROPER MENU, MOOD MUSIC, AND THE PERFECT COCKTAIL. OF COURSE, YOUR OWN PERSONAL FLAIR CAN TAKE IT FROM THERE.

MOST IMPORTANTLY, YOUR EQUATORIAL GALA IS BEST ENJOYED WITH PLENTY OF LAID-BACK ISLAND ATTITUDE. IF YOU WOULD RATHER SAMBA THAN SAUTÉ IN THE KITCHEN, CONSIDER CATERING OR FAST AND EASY TAKEOUT. WHETHER FEELING THE URGE TO TRANCE DANCE IN A SARONG, TANGO WITH A DAIQUIRI, OR JUST DRUM ON BONGOS ALL NIGHT, AN ISLAND PARTY IN FULL SWING WILL FIRE UP EVEN THE MOST SUBDUED REVELER.

IT'S MY PARTY AND I'LL MIX IF I WANT TO

Regardless of your theme, every party requires a bit of planning and panache to make certain that you're free to limbo.

STOCK THE FREEZER WITH PREMADE ICE

Ice is probably the least expensive and most essential item to have on hand. No need to run out midparty: cram your freezer full with the cold stuff and keep those fabulous drinks chilled.

PREP YOUR PARTY

You've run out of lime juice and are desperately juicing citrus while a conga-sized line impatiently grows at the bar. To avoid a similar scenario, have all the ingredients prepared before your first guest arrives.

AN ICE BUCKET WITH TONGS

While some consider an ice bucket and tongs to be a minor detail, this sleek icon of the cocktail presentation is actually fundamental to a successful party—as much a part of the functional equation as the cocktail shaker. An elegant ice bucket and tongs sidesteps the issue of guests having to grab a handful of freezing, wet cubes for themselves.

GLASSWARE

If you can make room in the freezer and refrigerator, prechilled glasses add frosty elegance to your libations. For large parties, a restaurant-supply store will have an extensive selection of glassware in various styles and large quantities for affordable prices.

A VARIETY OF REFRESHMENTS

Remember that while many of your guests will revel in the rum, some will choose not to indulge. To keep everyone's thirsts quenched, stock the bar with plenty of nonalcoholic beverages such as sparkling water, Jamaican ginger beer, and a variety of juices.

TOO MUCH OF A GOOD THING

Of course, your party will be considered the event of the season, but remember at evening's end, some of your guests' decidedly cheerful dispositions may be the result of enjoying too many spirited concoctions, rather than your festive surroundings. Call a cab for anyone who doesn't know a car key from a church key.

Cubisimo Cocktail Party

Prior to the 1950s, Havana was the hottest spot for wealthy Americans to flock when seeking a little exotica. The balmy weather, colorful Latin culture, countless casinos, and indulgent tropical libations drew glamorous *turistas* ninety miles south of Florida to spoil themselves senseless in the sun. That was the old Cuba: perfume-misted nights, mambo kings playing songs of love, and spinning worlds of rhythmic motion.

Hot. Steamy. Moving to the beat. That's what a Cuban party is all about. Creating your own Little Havana is as simple as filling your event with the most literary, artistic, intellectual, and pseudo-intellectual friends you can assemble. Tell them to bring their 1950s Chevys and DeSotos, to drag out their Che Guevara T-shirts, and to be prepared to drink until dawn. Depending on the season and location of your party, you can go "expatriate American" style with vintage cocktail dresses and tuxes or, equally appropriate, linen and seersucker.

LIBATION:
MY MANDARIN FROM HAVANA

A frozen daiquiri made with silver rum and a medley of citrus flavors and strained the El Floridita way for a frosty Cuban cocktail.

- **1 cup (8 ounces) good-quality silver rum**
- **3 ounces Mandarine Napoléon (mandarin liqueur)**
- **4 ounces fresh tangerine or mandarin juice**
- **2 ounces fresh lime juice**
- **2 tablespoons superfine sugar**
- **2 cups crushed ice**
- **4 small thin lime slices for garnish**

1. Chill four 6-ounce cocktail glasses.

2. In a blender, combine the rum, Mandarine Napoléon, tangerine and lime juices, sugar, and ice. Blend until well combined and slushy.

3. Using a fine-mesh metal strainer, slowly strain the mixture into the chilled glasses, dividing it evenly. Float a lime slice on top of each drink and serve.

Serves 4

102

INVITATIONS

Wrap your small but colorful handwritten invitation around a cigar, rewrapping the cigar band around the outside of the note. Send the invitations out in small cigar boxes or mailing tubes.

WHAT TO SERVE

Mini roast-pork sandwiches
Fried plantains
Grilled shrimp

WHAT TO PUT ON THE HI-FI

Buena Vista Social Club
Orishas (Cuban hip-hop)
Xavier Cugat
Dizzy Gillespie (Cuban period)
The Best of Tito Puente

ISLAND AMBIENCE

To recapture the essence of old Cuba, rent a few conga drums, dim the overheads, and place low-voltage lighting behind a few palms for dramatic tropical shadows. If you have a ceiling fan, set it on low and slow, for that quintessential gentle breeze and creaking sound effect that will transport you straight to the El Floridita bar.

ISLAND EFFECTS

While Cuban cigars are difficult to obtain in the States, get the thought across by filling colorful cigar boxes with stogies and placing the boxes throughout party headquarters. Be sure to provide the proper accoutrements (cigar cutters, lighters, ashtrays) so that your guests can partake . . . or just pose.

The night won't be authentic without some action on the dance floor. To avoid the "don't do mambo" syndrome, hire a duo of Latin dance instructors to jump-start your guests. With a little professional encouragement, your partygoers will be turning a mean rumba before you can say *cha cha cha.*

Balinese Soirée

While most of your tropical fetes will boast a high-pitched, celebratory tone, this low-profile soirée is perfect for your favorite crowd of elegant cool cats. Turn the lights down low, drape yourself in a silk sarong, and get ready for a serene scene.

LIBATION: PLUM-MANGO LASSI

A refined smoothie with a pan-Pacific edge, this luscious combination of fresh mango and plum is an Indonesian fusion of fruits, spices, and the essence of almond.

1 1/2 **cups vanilla yogurt**
1 **cup (8 ounces) mango nectar, chilled**
1 **mango, peeled, pitted, and cubed**
2 **small plums, peeled, pitted, and cubed**
1/4 **teaspoon orgeat or other almond-flavored syrup**
1/8 **teaspoon ground cardamom**
1/8 **teaspoon ground cloves**
1 **cup crushed ice**
4 **mango slices for garnish**

1. *Chill four 10- to 12-ounce glasses.*

2. *In a blender, combine the yogurt, mango nectar, cubed mango, plums, orgeat, cardamom, and cloves. Blend until well combined. Add the ice and blend until smooth.*

3. *Pour the mixture into the chilled glasses, dividing it evenly. Balance a mango slice on each rim and serve.*

Serves 4

INVITATIONS

Call your local florist and order short, round, fresh palm leaves. Using a silver- or gold-paint pen, write out the invitation information on the leaves and send out in elongated envelopes made with unbleached handmade paper or with decorative gold-leaf accents.

WHAT TO SERVE

Curried-coconut chicken skewers
Fresh vegetable spring rolls
Grilled basil-and-ginger marinated shrimp

WHAT TO PUT ON THE HI-FI

Balinese gamelan music

ISLAND AMBIENCE

Colorful patterned paper lanterns adorn all overhead or wall lighting, shedding a rosy glow in which your guests can bask. Envelop your guests with the intoxicating fragrances of frangipani or tuberose floral arrangements. To increase the exotic ambience, set up large Balinese umbrellas over low teak tables and procure a few large silk or batik floor pillows for lounging and soaking up the scene.

Serve the appetizers on trays covered with decorative patterned gold-leaf paper. Set up a display of fresh fruits similar to the Indonesian fruit shrines. Pass around a silver box of hand-rolled cigarettes for guests who wish to indulge.

ISLAND EFFECTS

Rent some treasures of percussion and let your guests rhythmically gong the night away.

Polynesian Spa Party

So, the girls have had a rough week and it's time to get together for a good, old-fashioned vent fest. Recognizing that it's tough to unload all of your personal dramas in the middle of a noisy bar, it's time for you to take action and treat your favorite gals to an afternoon of pampering, Polynesian style.

LIBATIONS:
I DREAM OF JEANNIE MARTINI

Straight from the Beauty Bar, that East Village hot spot on the island of Manhattan, comes this fabulous concoction from master mixologist Lara Turchinsky, with a nod to that mischievous South Seas beauty in her bottle.

- **1 tray ice cubes (14 to 16)**
- **6 ounces Malibu rum**
- **4 ounces Stolichnaya lemon vodka**
- **4 ounces Cointreau**
- **6 ounces cranberry juice**
- **2 ounces fresh lime juice**
- **4 lemon-peel twists (see page 20) for garnish**

1. Chill 4 large cocktail glasses.

2. Fill a large cocktail pitcher with the ice and add the rum, vodka, Cointreau, cranberry juice, and lime juice. Stir to blend and chill.

3. Pour the mixture into the chilled glasses, dividing it evenly. Twist a lemon peel over each glass, drop it in, and serve.

Serves 4

INVITATIONS

Frankly, you don't have time to send out elaborate invitations, and your equally busy girlfriends are never home to receive them anyway. Visit www.evite.com and create an e-mail invitation with a tropical theme that will get the girls ready to be spoiled.

WHAT TO SERVE

Grilled ahi tuna or salmon with a soy-ginger-lime marinade

Stir-fried bok choy and shiitake mushrooms

Fresh tropical fruit sliced and served with vanilla-honey yogurt or coconut sorbet

WHAT TO PUT ON THE HI-FI

Tropical nature tapes. Sounds of the seashore, rain forest, and sea breezes.

Yo Yo Ma's *Traditional Japanese Melodies*

Bebel Gilberto's *Tanto Tempo*

ISLAND AMBIENCE

Fill your abode with as many fresh flowers and aromatherapy candles as you can budget. These elements will be the key to whisking away your guests' imaginations to an island oasis.

Provide each guest with a bag of tropical spa toiletries such as mud masks, sea-salt sloughs, and seaweed wraps. Spend the afternoon indulging one another and recouping a new attitude.

ISLAND EFFECTS

Upon arrival, give each guest her own terrycloth robe and slippers to don for the afternoon. Hire a manicurist and/or masseuse to visit your home to deliver the island-princess treatment.

Urban Luau Madness

When the sun is beating down on your urban abode, it's time to invite the gang over to create your own faux-tropical fresh breezes. This is a sultry, primitive affair, with tiki torches, palm fronds, sarongs and sunbathing attire, and garlands of hibiscuses. All tropical clichés are acceptable, so you may choose to go subtle and elegant or full-on tiki. If you are lucky enough to have a patio or yard, veranda or balcony, push this soirée out into the balmy breezes.

LIBATION: SOUTH SEAS SANGRIA

This light and summery sangria infuses white wine with delicately fragrant tropical fruits. The spiciness of cloves, the orange essence of Grand Marnier, and the warm tones of brandy add depth and complexity. A dry white wine that has a light, crisp bouquet, such as Pinot Grigio or a white Rioja, is best here. This recipe can be prepared ahead of time. Let it chill overnight and serve the following day.

1 **pineapple, peeled, cored, and sliced**

2 **mangoes, peeled, pitted, and sliced**

1 **star fruit, sliced**

½ **cantaloupe, peeled, seeded, and cubed**

2 **nectarines, pitted and sliced**

1 **tangerine or small orange, quartered and sliced**

1 **lemon, quartered and sliced**

20 **whole cloves**

2 **ounces Grand Marnier**

2 **ounces brandy**

3 **tablespoons superfine sugar**

2 **bottles (750 ml each) white wine**

About 6 cups ice cubes

1. *In a large (at least 2-quart) glass pitcher, combine the pineapple, mangoes, star fruit, cantaloupe, nectarines, tangerine, and lemon. Sprinkle in the cloves.*

2. *In a mixing glass, stir together the Grand Marnier, brandy, and sugar until the sugar is dissolved. Add this mixture to the fruit, and stir gently to combine.*

3. *Slowly stir in the white wine.*

4. *Cover and refrigerate for at least 2 hours or as long as overnight to chill.*

5. *Fill tall 10-ounce glasses or wine goblets with ice cubes and pour the sangria over the ice.*

Serves 8 to 10

Variation: For a cooler that's light and bubbly, fill a glass halfway with the sangria and top off with club soda.

INVITATIONS

Send homemade hidden-treasure maps on parchment paper.
Your apartment is X-marks-the-spot.

WHAT TO SERVE

Sushi takeout from your favorite local Japanese restaurant
Skewered shrimp with mango-habanero glaze
An abundance of fresh tropical fruits

WHAT TO PUT ON THE HI-FI

Cape Verde (a Putumayo world music compilation)
Bing Crosby's "Bali Hai"
Harry Belafonte's *Calypso*
Yma Sumac's *Legend of the Sun Virgin*
Hukilau hulas music

ISLAND AMBIENCE

Set up a few patio torches, fill a kiddie pool with water and floating hibiscuses for toe dipping, and, to go all out, lay down a few rows of fresh sod if your yard is a fifth-floor balcony.

Fill your house with fans to emulate the cool sea breezes of the Caribbean. Again, as with most tropical parties, exotic floral and fauna are a welcome addition. Place bamboo votives strategically for a low-light mood. Arm your guests with colorful water spritzers and let them mist themselves silly. Hang a hammock or two for languid lounging.

Cover the buffet table with several yards of burlap to create a primitive-island effect. Coconut-shell cups (see page 20) are a given here. Empty wooden crates begged from your local grocery store double as great guest seating.

ISLAND EFFECTS

As your guests arrive for the festivities, decorate them with fresh leis. Set the scene by popping *South Pacific* or Elvis's *Blue Hawaii* into the VCR. Bring out the island artist in your guests: have on hand miniature black-velvet canvases and pastel oil sticks so they can experience the Gauguin-like inspiration of primitivism to create mini masterpieces.

Tropical Tango for Two

It's the dead of winter and the dinner-and-a-movie approach to your relationship is losing its mystique. Invite your sweetie over for a weekend getaway, but opt to travel only to the land of love.

LIBATION: PASSION-FRUIT COCKTAIL

Add a bit of passion to that romantic Champagne for two with this heady combination of passion fruit and a splash of the bubbly, for the euphoric mingling of sultry fruit and effervescence.

2	**passion fruits**
6 to 8	**ounces Champagne, chilled**
2	**small tea-rose petals for garnish**

1. Chill 2 Champagne flutes.

2. Cut the passion fruits in half and squeeze the juice of 1 fruit into each chilled glass.

3. Slowly fill each glass with the Champagne. Float a rose petal in each glass to garnish, then serve.

Serves 2

INVITATIONS

You only have one guest, so splurge on the invite! Send your special someone exotic flowers on Thursday afternoon with the warning that the heat will be turned up in twenty-four hours.

WHAT TO SERVE

Caviar with the traditional garnishes

Raw oysters on ice

Cinnamon French toast with peach-mango compote

WHAT TO PUT ON THE HI-FI

Any Astor Piazzolla CD
    (the Argentinean tango master)
Gabriela Anders's *Wanting*

ISLAND AMBIENCE

Use only low votive candlelight of course. Make a canopy of fine muslin netting that hangs from the ceiling like a tent and surrounds an intimately set table. Complete the setting with palm fronds or potted palms in the corners of the space, and have exotic flowers on the table.

ISLAND EFFECTS

Rent the 1975 Italian classic *Swept Away* and imagine yourselves stranded from civilization with a great tan. Bring out that aromatic bottle of coconut-scented suntan oil to capture that *From Here to Eternity* moment on the beach.

Index

Index

Table of Equivalents

The exact equivalents in the following tables have been rounded for convenience.

LIQUID/DRY MEASURES

U.S.	Metric
1/4 teaspoon	1.25 milliliters
1/2 teaspoon	2.5 milliliters
1 teaspoon	5 milliliters
1 tablespoon (3 teaspoons)	15 milliliters
1 fluid ounce (2 tablespoons)	30 milliliters
1/4 cup	60 milliliters
1/3 cup	80 milliliters
1/2 cup	120 milliliters
1 cup	240 milliliters
1 pint (2 cups)	480 milliliters
1 quart (4 cups, 32 ounces)	960 milliliters
1 gallon (4 quarts)	3.84 liters
1 ounce (by weight)	28 grams
1 pound	454 grams
2.2 pounds	1 kilogram

LENGTH

U.S.	Metric
1/8 inch	3 millimeters
1/4 inch	6 millimeters
1/2 inch	12 millimeters
1 inch	2.5 centimeters

OVEN TEMPERATURE

Fahrenheit	Celsius	Gas
250	120	1/2
275	140	1
300	150	2
325	160	3
350	180	4
375	190	5
400	200	6
425	220	7
450	230	8
475	240	9
500	260	10